From Sea to Sea

A Personal Journey

Min-Hwa Cheng Kennard

ARCHWAY PUBLISHING

Copyright © 2022 Min-Hwa Cheng Kennard.

All rights reserved. No part of this book may be used or reproduced by any means, graphic, electronic, or mechanical, including photocopying, recording, taping or by any information storage retrieval system without the written permission of the author except in the case of brief quotations embodied in critical articles and reviews.

Archway Publishing books may be ordered through booksellers or by contacting:

Archway Publishing
1663 Liberty Drive
Bloomington, IN 47403
www.archwaypublishing.com
844-669-3957

Because of the dynamic nature of the Internet, any web addresses or links contained in this book may have changed since publication and may no longer be valid. The views expressed in this work are solely those of the author and do not necessarily reflect the views of the publisher, and the publisher hereby disclaims any responsibility for them.

Any people depicted in stock imagery provided by Getty Images are models, and such images are being used for illustrative purposes only. Certain stock imagery © Getty Images.

ISBN: 978-1-6657-1459-4 (sc)
ISBN: 978-1-6657-1460-0 (e)

Library of Congress Control Number: 2021922825

Print information available on the last page.

Archway Publishing rev. date: 12/22/2021

In loving memory of my parents

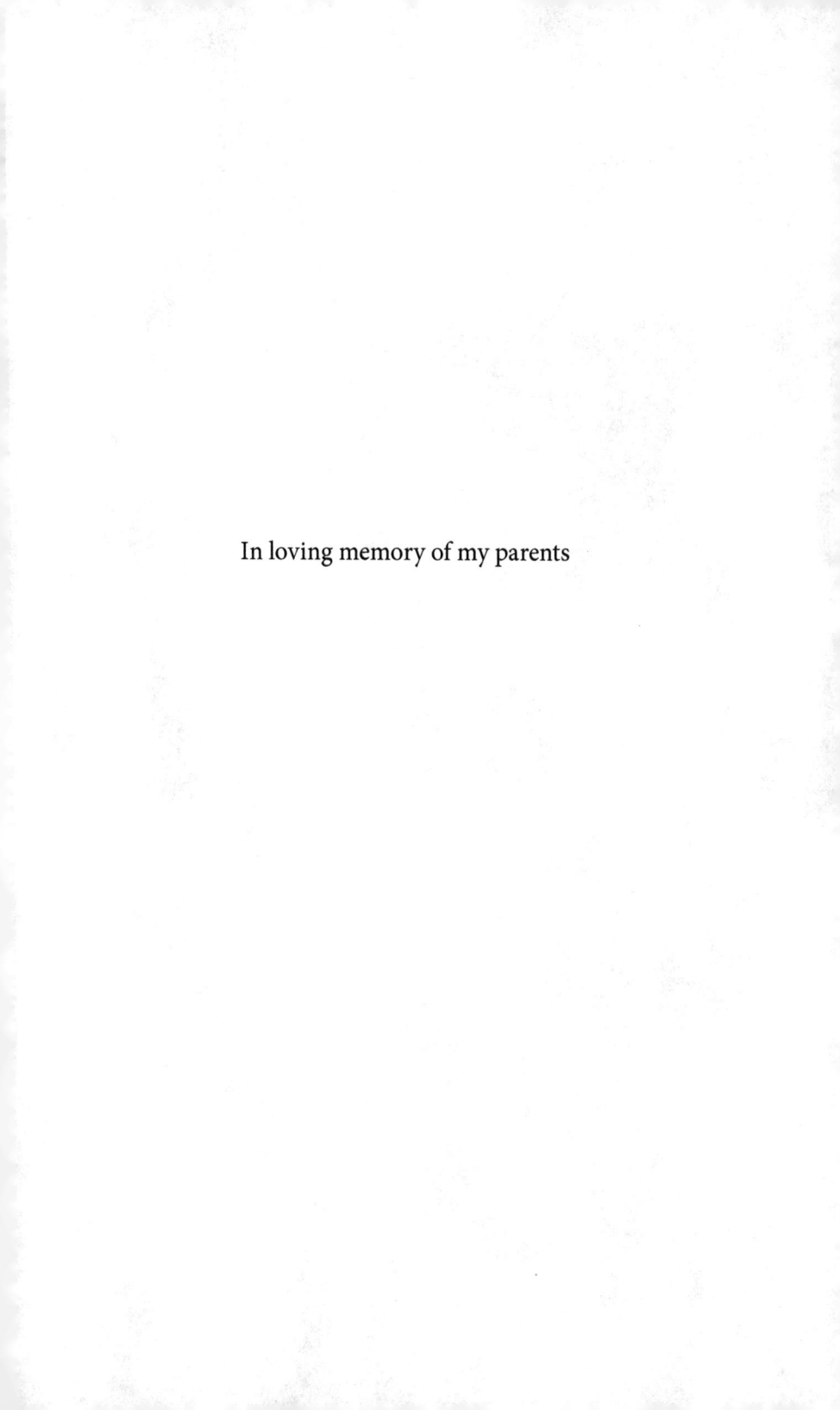

Contents

My Mother's Wedding 1
In Search of the Childhood Homes 17
Reunion 33
Mother's Illness 39
Journey to the Sea 43
Two Rochelles 56
The Long Road to Recovery 64
Sweetest Love, Do Not Go 70
Two Paintings 75
Dajie and Me 82
Seven Lunch Boxes 101
Grandmother's Food Wagon 106
Tiny Tears 110
He Is the One 115
The Little Red House and Other Things Too 118
I Cast a Last Glance from #2210 121
The Project 123
Letter from Jakarta 132
Out of the End of the World 139
Pakistan Diary 145

My Mother's Wedding

It is a well-known family "secret" that my mother married my father against her family's wishes.

My parents met during the Sino-Japanese War (1937–1945), when my mother lived with her older brother and his family in Lanzhou, a city in Northwest China. After a brief courtship, my parents were engaged to be married. For some reason, my father did not get along with his future brother-in-law. Nevertheless, my mother married my father.

As a child growing up in Taiwan, I loved to retrieve the photo albums from my mother's private closet and browse family photos from a bygone era. The only wedding picture of my parents was a yellowing black-and-white photo, a bit smaller than half a page in landscape orientation. The bride and the groom stand in the middle of a small group of guests in front of a restaurant. She is in a dark knee-length Chinese dress, and he wears a formal Zhongshan suit. Both look solemn and reserved, which was probably typical for photo posing in that era. I once asked Mother who those people were. Before she uttered a single word, her eyes turned red. I never asked the same question again. Instead, I managed to find out what had happened: no one in my mother's family attended her wedding, and she and her brother never met again after she was married.

When my mother died, I was fifteen, still too young and immature to share an intimate rapport with her. I knew very little about her beyond her being our mother. Decades later, having lived beyond her age, I realized what a loss it was not to know more about my mother's tragically short life. What kind of life did she live before her marriage? Why did she go to the northwest of China from her hometown on the east coast? Why did she marry my father despite her family's objections?

During the transition leading up to the Communist takeover of the Chinese mainland in 1949, my parents moved our family to Taiwan. My mother's maternal family remained on the mainland. For thirty years, all exchanges between China and Taiwan were cut off. I thought I would never find the answers to my questions, and that my mother's past had been long buried in a different world.

Then China opened its doors to the world.

In 1982, twenty-two years after my mother's passing, her brother, whom we referred to as "Da Jiujiu" ("Big Uncle"), visited his daughter (my cousin, Ming) in San Francisco. The timing happened to coincide with my father's trip to Los Angeles, where my brothers and sisters lived. Urged by all of us, Father phoned his brother-in-law at Ming's. According to one witness, their conversation went well. Father asked about his half-brothers-in-law: Kui, Jia, and Lo. Yet this episode brought Father a renewed sense of loss and emotional turmoil. Struck by a sudden surge of grief and anger, neither Father nor Big Uncle took the initiative to meet with each other. Later that year, Father died.

After that initial contact, I looked forward to keeping up with the renewed family connection that had been broken four decades earlier. A year later, my husband and I went to China on a lecturing tour. We met Big Uncle in Xi'an and had a good time touring the ancient city and, more importantly, getting to know each other. He mentioned my brothers and sisters, whom he had met during his last visit to San Francisco.

I asked my uncle if he saw our mother in any of us. Without hesitation, he replied, "Your mom spoke with poise and reserve; you guys talk like shooting rifles." He then added, "Your mother and I both had curly hair, the unique feature of the Qiu family. What a pity that none of you got it!" "Oh well," I thought, "in Big Uncle's eyes none of us was worthy of his sister, and deep down inside he still has misgivings about her bad choice." On the contrary, it always struck me how proud my father was of our resemblance to our mother. When he met my children for the first time, he said, "Look! Your baby girl has her grandma's ears; the boy's eyebrows are as straight as a pair of swords, typical of the Qiu family!"

Apart from that, Big Uncle talked about my mother's horsemanship with high praise. I had never seen my mother ride a horse. For us, she was a housewife all her life. It was impossible to conjure up an image of her as a young girl in Western riding attire, galloping over the causeway across the West Lake. But that was her, my own mother. Now some of the stories my mother had told came back to me: "One time, as I was riding by an empty field, my horse refused to proceed, no matter how much I cajoled her. Later I found out that area had been used for executions during the late dynasty. You know, horses have special senses and can see things we humans can't." Through my uncle, I was beginning to see my mother as a different person.

Unfortunately, only a few years after that trip, Big Uncle in China and Cousin Ming in San Francisco passed away. My mother's story remained in the deep recesses of my mind, like an unfinished piece of music.

In the spring of 1994, during a business trip to China, I had a chance to visit my mother's hometown in Hangzhou. There, I met Cousin Mao, one of Big Uncle's three children. From him I learned a great deal about the family. I also met three of my mother's half-brothers. With each additional acquaintance, I collected more information that helped me sketch a basic account of my mother's early life.

Grandfather and Big Uncle

When I was growing up, my siblings and I were told that our maternal grandfather, Qiu Ji Shen, was a renowned doctor in traditional Chinese medicine. In my childhood house, there was a set of medical encyclopedia that had been compiled and edited by my grandfather. The entire set consisted of twenty-four volumes, all covered with faded blue-gray cloth. It was first published in 1936 in Shanghai, and then went out of print during the eight years of the war (1937–1945). By sheer luck, my father came across a complete set in a used book shop and bought it. The books stayed with the family as we moved from Shanghai to Taiwan as part of the essential household belongings. Later, in Taiwan, my father donated the copyright to a local publisher in honor of my grandfather's aspiration to benefit the public with his medical work. The entire set of my grandfather's work was reissued in 1961 in recognition of its intrinsic and historical value. When I visited Taiwan in 1989, this twenty-four-volume encyclopedia had long been out of print. I managed to find the only copy left in the warehouse of the publisher and brought it back to the States. Since then, I have taken it with me to wherever I lived, even abroad.

My grandfather didn't start his career as a medical doctor. Instead, he had dedicated his early years to the revolution to oust the monarchy. My maternal grandmother had two children, Da Jiujiu (Big Uncle) and our mother, Qiu Shi Fu. Big Uncle was born in northeast China when my grandparents were still involved in the revolution. Grandfather was one of the founding members of the Alliance League, the predecessor of the Revolutionary Party led by Dr. Sun Yat-sen. My grandmother (née Chen) befriended the famous revolutionary martyr, Lady Qiu Jin. Grandmother was the one who removed Qiu Jin's body after her execution to escape any posthumous retribution by the Qing monarch.

After the republic was founded, the family moved back to their hometown of Shaoxing in Zhejiang province, where Grandfather started his medical practice. As the only daughter of an elderly couple, my mother was adored like a "shiny pearl in the palm." Before she started school, the family moved to Hangzhou, where Grandfather founded San San Hospital.

I saw my mother's childhood home on a trip in 1994 when I visited Hangzhou for the first time. Cousin Mao took me to the compound that used to be the hospital. Located on the southeast side of West Lake adjacent to the city center, it was a U-shaped two-story Western style building with a tower. Standing on top of it was a bronze stork. At the time of my visit, the entire building was used as a day care center with dorm rooms for the staff. Cousin Mao and I managed to get into the building and saw my mother's room on the second floor facing the cobblestoned courtyard. In the left wing of the building, we also found the original stable that had housed the family carriage and horses decades earlier.

As a child, Big Uncle loved horses, and he and Mother took riding lessons. During that trip, Cousin Mao gave me a copy of a picture of them in their handsome riding suits and boots walking their horses up an alleyway. I could almost hear the horses' hooves click-clacking on the cobblestones of yesteryear.

My maternal grandmother died when my mother was not yet eleven and her brother seventeen. Her brother's wife, four years older than her husband, took on the responsibility of caring for my mother; such was the usual arrangement in a household where three generations lived together. After Grandfather remarried, the household split into two: one under Grandfather and the other under my uncle, the son of the family. Cousin Mao said, "Niang Niang (a nickname for *aunt*) was an integral part of our early life. There was not a single day when I didn't have her around."

Unfortunately, Big Uncle's wife died after giving birth to three babies in three consecutive years. Though my uncle soon remarried, my mother stayed in his household as her brother's most trusted friend and personal assistant. For his three children, Ming, Mao, and Hui, she played a dual role of an aunt and a big sister. Cousin Mao recalled, "Niang Niang was always there for us. If we got sick, she would spend all night with us. When school started, Niang Niang would make book covers for our new books, and she made sure that our lunch boxes were properly prepared. If we needed anything, we would go to her first. As short-tempered as my father was, he was always gentle with his sister." When Big Uncle moved to Shanghai for medical school, my mother went along as part of the family.

After completing his MD and requisite medical training, Big Uncle and his family, including my mother, returned to Hangzhou, where he joined Grandfather's practice as one of the medical staff. My mother didn't continue her formal schooling; instead, she worked with Grandfather as one of his assistants. After several years, she was knowledgeable enough to treat common illnesses. My grandfather spent most of his time compiling the medical encyclopedia, and my mother was part of his editorial team on nine of the subjects in his voluminous work.

Before the war, Grandfather's medical practice was thriving, and the family lived a comfortable lifestyle. If someone fancied a snack from Cai Zhi Zai, a famous Shanghai deli some 150 miles away, they could have the order delivered to Hangzhou on the same day. As a great fan of Beijing Opera, Big Uncle took opera singing lessons from renowned singers, and he included my mother in his pursuit of operatic art. In a few years, they became accomplished enough to give performances to the public and on the radio. My mother's half-brother, Jia, recalled Big Uncle and Mother performing the opera *Return to the Court*, during which my mother, as the queen mother, sang the entire act in a sitting position. From Cousin Mao, I also got a picture of her in costume playing the lead role in the opera *The Lantern of Precious Lotus*.

What a shame that my mother never furthered her artistic interests after her marriage! She was not only too occupied by her family responsibilities but also discouraged by Father's disparaging attitude toward all such "bourgeois pursuits." Yet, over the years of their marriage, he himself grew very fond of the Beijing Opera, obviously because of my mother's influence. Whenever a popular singer was in town, Father would make a great effort to get the best tickets for the performance. Occasionally, if I did well at school, I would be rewarded with an outing to the theater with my parents, even though in most instances I fell asleep halfway through the opera. From those childhood experiences, I have acquired a deep affection for the Beijing Opera. Whenever I hear the Beijing Opera music, whether it is on the street, on TV, or on the radio, the songs and acts instantly transport me back to my childhood.

Journey to the Northwest

The Sino-Japanese War changed every aspect of life in China. At the onset of the war, Japanese military action was focused on cities along the coast, especially the triangular area between Shanghai, Nanjing, and Hangzhou. In 1937, in view of the imminent danger, Grandfather and Big Uncle split the family into two camps: Grandfather and his second wife took the younger children to the countryside while Big Uncle, his second wife, and my mother along with the older children went westward to the areas the

Japanese had not yet reached. This trip turned out to be a three-year odyssey.

My uncle and his family went first to Jiangxi province, where he took a position as the acting director of a military hospital. Unfortunately, less than a year later the Japanese military expansion had reached far enough to make that locale unsafe. My uncle received orders to move the entire hospital to the adjacent Hunan province. After a journey of days and weeks with a large hospital staff and heavy equipment, and just as they were settled in the new location, ferocious Japanese bombing caught up with them. One morning while Cousin Ming was walking to school, the siren blasted. She immediately turned back but the bombing had already started. All by herself, she took shelter wherever she could while creeping slowly toward home. By the time she got home, half of the city had been reduced to rubble. No one knew how many children out there were among the casualties of that bombing.

Once again, my uncle had to mobilize the entire hospital for yet another journey to a city farther south in Hunan. This time they took the river instead of the road. For the children it was a change from the tortuous bus ride on rough roads. On the way to the new destination, they witnessed the infamous Changsha Incident of 1938. This is what Cousin Mao, who was eight then, remembered:

> We kids had already gone to bed that night. All of a sudden, someone saw red flames raging on the opposite side of the river. Instantly, the speculation that the Japanese had taken Changsha spread like wildfire among the passengers. My father, as the director of the hospital, ordered the staff to get on shore urgently to bypass Changsha, and under such circumstances, most heavy equipment and

extra supplies must be abandoned by the road. Niang Niang had to let go of truckloads of fancy dresses. Walking on foot during the day, sleeping on haystacks at night for a few days, we just couldn't move any farther. Finally, they hired a bamboo sedan chair for Niang Niang and me. With the gentle rocking of the chair, I quickly fell asleep in her arms.

When the group reached the next town, they learned that the fire had been instigated by the local government, aimed at deterring the Japanese air attacks. As a result, the entire city was turned into ashes with countless civilian casualties—a hellish scene.

After that incident, my uncle set his sights on the northwest part of the country, which was beyond the reach of the Japanese military. He secured a position in the provincial health department in Lanzhou, the major city in the northwest, on the corridor leading to the ancient Silk Road. So, the family was to embark on another journey.

They covered some of the most difficult terrain in China, including Yungui Plateau, Sichuan Basin, and northwest Loess. Throughout the journey, they were besieged from time to time by enemy bombs. They finally arrived at the destination in the fall of 1939, more than two years later. This journey not only brought my mother from the east coast of China to the northwest; it also changed her entire life.

Meeting

Lanzhou is a city in a valley of the Yellow River, long and narrow and hemmed in by mountains.

Since ancient times it had been one of the gateways of China, the last place one could change horses and buy provisions before heading for the outer limits of the empire. The mountains were bare and stony. The river was so shallow that there was no boat on it larger than a sampan.

In the beginning of the Sino-Japanese War, my father was assigned by the Nationalist government to Lanzhou, to work on economic planning for the provincial governments. Later, he was appointed the special inspector and director of security of the Third War Zone. At thirty-six, he was one of the most eligible bachelors in Lanzhou social circles. Many decades later, my parents' friends still commented, "Your dad was very picky; he turned down practically every young lady available in Lanzhou before he met your mother."

Due to the long journey and the extraordinary time of the war, my mother was still unmarried at twenty-four, which was considered older than the norm for marriage. Through a common friend in Lanzhou, my parents met. He was seriously attracted to her gentle demeanor and poise, and she was swept away by his talents and wit, and found him irresistible. The romance went well in the beginning. He would visit her in her brother's house, sometimes on horseback. To his surprise, she was well trained in riding when she commented, "It is a good horse and a gentle one, otherwise it would flip over an inexperienced rider like you."

One of their favorite outings was to ride the goatskin raft on the Yellow River floating down the torrents at great speed. On one of the rides, the besotted man asked his beloved lady to sing an opera aria for him. Though she was reluctant because she thought she had lost her voice during the long journey, my mother was finally persuaded by her irresistible suitor. Sitting upright, with delicate gestures and a playful expression, she sang "The Drinking

Song of Consort Yang." Every note was a tender and yearning message to his ear. How my father's heart was overflowing with feelings while my mother's singing floated downstream past the rocks and currents!

My parents came from two very different backgrounds. If it weren't for the war, they would never have met, let alone married. He was from the countryside of Jiangxi, one of the poorest provinces in East China. Having lost his father at fourteen, my father had to make his life and career with a lot of effort and endurance. Moreover, from a very tender age, he was one of the two oldest sons supporting an entire family, including his younger siblings' education. That was probably why he was still single at thirty-six. My mother, on the other hand, as the only daughter of a privileged family, had comfortable formative years and never had to work outside the home. Instead, she worked with Grandfather on his medical encyclopedia and became well versed in traditional medicine herself. Despite all, their marriage was quickly agreed to by all parties concerned.

Once engaged to my mother, my father was a regular guest in my uncle's house. Yet my father and my uncle didn't really see eye to eye. Coming from a tough background, my father couldn't hide his contempt toward someone from the "East Coast establishment." And this misgiving was coupled with the fact that he was older and more experienced than his future brother-in-law. On the other hand, Big Uncle considered himself not only the elder brother but also the family representative of his sister. In his eyes, my father lacked refinement, even though he was one of the few who had been selected by the government to study abroad.

Eventually the undercurrent of misgivings bubbled up. One day, after a dinner party in the house, my mother retired to her room due to a minor illness while the rest of the family and guests carried on with the conversation. My uncle's wife casually cracked a joke with my father, which was unfortunately taken by her husband as flirting. "How shameless you are!" he snapped at his wife. But my father took it as an insult directed toward himself. He went into a rage and pounced on the host. That started a fight, which continued with increasing fierceness. In a fit of passion, Father pulled out a pistol that he had been given for his job. If it hadn't been for the timely intervention of another guest, the resulting situation would have been unthinkable!

According to Mao, after that incident, not surprisingly, my father was banned from Big Uncle's house, and all the wedding arrangements were called off. What a devastating blow to my poor mother! She lost weight and fell seriously ill, to the point of coughing blood. "You will suffer more if you are married to such a horrid man!" her brother warned her starkly. The only one sympathetic to her was Big Uncle's daughter, Ming, who was then a middle school student. After the incident, my father managed to reach the girl after school and handed her a daily love letter for her aunt. (I couldn't find any of these letters in my mother's collections, but I know my father could express himself beautifully and powerfully in writing.) So, the romance went on secretly for a while until my uncle discovered the "conspiracy." He angrily accused his sister and daughter of being "traitors," a term not to be used lightly during the war. Bitter and hurt, my mother moved out of his house. No one in the family dared to ask about her or to find out where she went.

In the fall of that year (1940), my parents got married. No one from the bride's family attended the wedding. Sixty years later, I met one of the guests, Mrs. Huang, in Los Angeles. She told me that my mother's family had objected to the marriage because the groom was much too old for her, which seemed to me a pretext. Immediately after the wedding, the roof of the restaurant where the wedding banquet was held caved in. "I hope this is not a bad omen," Mother said with a sigh while looking at her own wedding photo. How uneasy she must have felt as she stepped into a new phase of her life! According to Cousin Mao, my uncle filed a lawsuit against my father for some sort of misdemeanor. Before long Big Uncle's family moved to another town, and no one knew what happened to the case.

Separation

As soon as the war was over, my mother, along with my father, and her brother visited their aging father in their hometown, but separately. The following year Grandfather passed away. Neither my mother, who was about to give birth to my younger brother, nor my uncle, who had just returned to his job in the northwest, could attend the funeral. My father rounded up Cousin Ming and Cousin Mao from Shanghai and took care of all the funeral logistics as well as the costs. My grandfather had lost his practice and all his property during the war, so he died a poor man. It was my father who took on the responsibility of supporting my mother's stepmother and two of her five half-brothers, who were still teenagers. A year later, Cousin Mao visited us in Nanjing. The moment he mentioned his father (Big Uncle), my mother's eyes filled with tears. "I had never seen Niang Niang so sad. I wrote to my father and asked him to reconcile with her. But he didn't like what I said."

In the ensuing years, the civil war between the Nationalist government and Communists intensified. Around the time the Communists took over China (1949), our family, along with Cousin Ming, left the mainland for Taiwan. During all those years in Taiwan, Cousin Ming was part of our family, and most importantly, the only connection between us and my mother's parental family. They spoke their hometown dialect between themselves. In the early years when we lived in Taiwan, many Communist pilots defected to Taiwan; Mother would carefully check the names published in the newspaper, hoping a familiar one would pop up like a miracle. Years later, Cousin Ming got news from her father via a connection in Hong Kong. This brought Mother a glimpse of hope that she would meet her family again. Yet, whenever Big Uncle's name was mentioned, Father would make derogatory comments, causing Mother a lot of grief.

Farewell

More than half a century has passed since the unfortunate incident that caused the rift between my father and Big Uncle. The parties involved are gone, along with the love and hate between them. Only deep regret remains.

Uncle Jia said, "The two of them didn't get along. Your mom, caught in the middle, suffered the most."

Uncle Lu said, "My brother had a terrible temper when he was young; he was much better in later years."

Cousin Mao said, "My father was too bogged down by this traditional mentality; he thought Niang Niang's decision to get married disrespected his authority as the older brother and the head of the family." He added, "If it weren't for the strong affection Niang Niang had for your father, she would never have done anything against her own brother's wishes. Understandably, my father's feelings were terribly hurt by her decision."

Recalling my brief encounter with my uncle in Xi'an twenty years before, I was struck by how much he and Father were alike: both were articulate and cultured, quick-tempered and stubborn. Perhaps that's why Mother fell for Father, as he represented the idol of her early life.

On the other hand, the two of them were very different in style and mentality. Father blamed my uncle for not doing his duty in nurturing my mother's talents and intellect. Given Father's demanding personality, it was not easy for Mother to be a wife and a mother, particularly without any family support. As I recall, when I was a junior in high school, I signed up for an English class at an evening school. To my surprise, Mother came with me and signed up for a class herself. She wanted to be the "ideal wife" of whom she thought Father would be proud. In fact, Father was very appreciative of Mother's being a good housewife. "Your mom had never stepped into a kitchen before marrying me," he said. "Now, not only does she make delicious meals every day, but she can also put together a banquet with ease."

Big Uncle suffered a lot due to the Cultural Revolution, yet he seemed practical enough to cope with the situation as it came. "During the Cultural Revolution, I was persecuted in public; I was made to parade around holding a board with humiliating language. But since I was a doctor, they always let me go back to work after those meetings." His biggest regret was that the Red Guards smashed his fine collection of Beijing Opera records.

My father, on the other hand, could be extremely moody and difficult to deal with as he went through ups and downs in his political career. Sometimes, Mother shed tears as she thought about her brother's advice: "You will suffer more if married to such a man!"

My mother fell ill when I was thirteen. As her illness proved to be incurable, she became even more homesick for her family. "My father was a traditional doctor; my brother a Western medical doctor," she said. "If only they were here! How I wish to have a dream of your grandfather; I'm sure he would give me a prescription for my illness."

Mother didn't want to leave us. "When your grandmother died, I was less than eleven; if I go now, Yao (my youngest sister) will only be ten." Father repaid her love by bringing up seven children, who were aged ten to nineteen when she died, as a single parent. And he remained alone for the last twenty-two years of his life.

> So many long years passed, and we are
> separated by the paths of living and dying.
> I try not to think, but I just can't forget.
> Toward the lone grave thousands of miles
> away, I can utter no words but sorrow.
> Even if we meet again, you wouldn't
> recognize me, as my face is covered with
> dust and my hair white like snow.
> Last night I dreamt of returning home; by the
> window you were grooming in the morning light.
> Not uttering a word, our tears
> flowed like a thousand rivers.
> Same day every year, I feel the
> same pain of parting.
> Under the moonlight, there are only
> short pine trees on the hill.
>
> —Su Shi (1037–1101)

In Search of the Childhood Homes

The Mystery of Two Houses and a Well

I was awakened from a deep sleep by a phone call. It was past midnight in the US East Coast. I picked up the phone and heard Ien's voice, "Ma, we are now in Shanghai, at Madame Soong's memorial museum." Ien and his girlfriend had been visiting her family in Shanghai and were now doing as I had asked, which was to positively identify the house my family had lived in many decades before.

For years, I had been told by family friends and relatives that our family used to live in the house that became the residence for Madame Soong, the widow of Dr. Sun Yat-sen, the founding father of the Republic of China. One of my very few early childhood memories associated with our Shanghai home was a well in the garden. To put these two pieces together, I asked Ien, "Is there a well in the backyard?"

The sound of busy steps came through the phone, followed by Ien's voice, "No, Ma! We have looked all over. I'm afraid there is no well."

"Could you find out when Madame Soong moved into her residence?"

"According to the museum guide, it was in 1948. If your family did live in this house, you must have already left Shanghai by then."

"I'm not sure when exactly my family left Shanghai, but one thing I know for sure is that we left the Chinese mainland from Shanghai. But if there is no well in the garden, it mustn't be the last house we lived in."

"But why would your relatives tell you that your family had lived in the house that turned into Madame Soong's Museum?"

"That is exactly the mystery I want to solve," I said. "We will get to the bottom of it, if at all possible."

~

My family were among the millions who moved to Taiwan from mainland China during the political transition between the Communist and the Nationalist governments, sometime around the end of 1948 and the beginning of 1949.

My memories of my early childhood in China consist mostly of scattered images, bordering on dreams and imagination. Yet a few episodes stand out with clear details, such as the well in the backyard.

> *It is a wintry day. There are snow flurries in the air. Some workers are working around an old well in the backyard. Mother asked them to check the well, making sure that we kids would not fall into it by accident. As I look inside the well, a young man is slowly descending by pushing his legs and arms against the inside wall. Once he reaches the bottom, he takes off his shirt and turns his head up, saying, "It is very warm down there."*

Of course, I could have mistaken those early memories with what I heard from my parents, family friends, and older siblings. It was only history, after all. I didn't think we would ever return to those places in our lifetime, or so I thought. Years went by silently. Our parents were no more, and the only thing left of them was what they had said that was vaguely imprinted on my subconscious. I was hit by an overwhelming sense of loss, a forgotten childhood, a precious world gone.

Since then, I have been in contact with my parents' relatives and friends who remained on the mainland after we left for Taiwan. Cousin Mao said Father lived in a big house on Avenue Joffre (known as Huaihai Road today). He believed it was the very house that eventually became Madame Soong's residence. "According to the photos on the Internet, the Soong Museum is a villa-type house, situated in the middle of a big garden. It looks very much like your house, and the address is also on Avenue Joffre." But Uncle Kui, one of my mother's half-brothers, who happened to work in Shanghai at that time, said our family home was in an alleyway, not on a major thoroughfare like Huaihai Road. This conflicting information prompted my request for Ien to search for our family home in Shanghai.

When China opened its doors decades after I had left the country, I went back to the cities where my family had lived to find out what had happened to my parents and our family during some of the country's most tumultuous years in the twentieth century. What I discovered, along with my scanty recollection of events, enabled me to track unknown details of my family history and to compose a portrait of how my family lived during that brief but pivotal era, when many events happened in a rather convoluted sequence, starting from my own birth in Chongqing.

Our Home in Nanjing

I was born in Chongqing, the wartime capital of China. The memory of early childhood didn't start until our family moved back to the east the year after the war ended. Before Shanghai, my family lived in Nanjing, then the capital of China, for a couple of years. During that time, my mother had two more babies, so we were six children altogether. The first event logged in my baby brain is being held on my father's shoulder while my mother was nursing a newborn, the little brother who was born when I was two.

> I was crying for my mom's attention, resisting going to sleep. My father broke the grip of my hands around my mother's neck, held me with one hand on his one shoulder, and patted my back with the other hand. Under the rhythmic pounding of a giant's warm palm, I calmed down and fell asleep.

My parents loved to call their Nanjing home "Zhong Nan Li" (Zhong-Nan Estate), with a nostalgic tone. My elder brothers and sister remembered their summer outings with the relatives to Xuan Wu Lake, where they picked lotus bulbs and horn-shaped nuts in the water. Even to this day, I feel a wave of nostalgia whenever I come across food stalls selling steaming hot lotus root nuts.

In early 2000 I went to Nanjing with my husband after a hiatus of five decades. I visited our home in Zhong Nan Li Estate, which I thought would not exist given all the changes that had occurred over the span of a half century. Upon arrival in Nanjing, we met Uncle Jia, one of my mother's half-brothers. He was very emotional when he saw me, after the titanic shift in the country and countless happenings in the family. "Your mother was very kind to me, something I will never forget," he said, with tears in his eyes. "When I first came to Nanjing from our hometown of Hangzhou, I had hardly anything, except for what I was wearing. She immediately bought me warm clothes and registered me at school." In 1946, Uncle Jia was only sixteen. He came to stay with us in Nanjing as my grandfather had become increasingly frail under the tough living conditions caused by the war.

Uncle Jia took us straight to Zhong Nan Li, a housing compound with hundreds of Western-style townhouses built in the early twentieth century. The overall appearance was somewhat derelict, with electrical cables, air conditioning units, and green awnings sticking out of the buildings. Uncle Jia told us that Zhong Nan Li was significant during the Chinese civil war as it was the headquarters from which the Nationalist government and the Communist representatives ran their intelligence operations.

From the front gate of the compound, we walked along the main alley flanked by houses of similar style. At the T-junction, we turned to the left, and again to the right. Our family home was the last unit on the right, a three-story house with three gables on the top floor. It had been divided into two units: the ground floor was occupied by one family, and the second and third floors housed another family. From the back door, which is used as the primary entryway, we entered the house and were led to a staircase. To the right of it was a kitchen/dining/bathroom combination replacing what had been our family kitchen. To the left, a hallway led to two rooms. The smaller room used to be the dining room and the bigger one the living room, separated from each other with a curtain. A glass cabinet used to stand in the dining room displaying Father's antique collections. Now both rooms were being used as bedrooms. Only the huge iron widow in the big room remained the same. The big room opened to a terrace, where my father used to park his chauffeured car. It was now an atrium-like living room. Uncle Jia's description of what he remembered about the house sounded strange to me between what was in the past and what was in the present.

On the second floor, the room to the right of the staircase was a kitchen and bathroom combination, converted from what had been a room for older children in our family. To the left, a hallway led to two rooms. The smaller one had been my father's study and the other was the master bedroom, which led to a small balcony. Uncle Jia said, "There was a bed in the study. That's where I slept when I stayed with your family."

The third floor had once been a big attic room for live-in maids, but it was divided into two rooms. There were two double beds in the big room, taking up almost the entire space. A long-buried image suddenly jumped out of my memory: several toddlers jumping back and forth between the two beds in the larger bedroom. As always, fighting between the "good" girls and "naughty" boys broke out. The energy and commotion were a spectacle for me as a toddler to behold.

My father was extraordinarily hospitable with friends and family, and the house was always full of people. My father's brother, whom we called "Big Uncle," stayed with us when we moved into the house.

Shortly after we were settled in Nanjing, my mother took the three eldest children to visit her father in Hangzhou. Sadly, I missed that trip, the only chance to meet my grandfather, as he died a year later. In a personal essay about Grandfather's death, Uncle Jia wrote:

> Before I returned home from Nanjing, I stopped by the hospital to visit my sister, who was about to give birth to a new baby. Even though I tried to act normally, she sensed the gravity of Father's illness

and cried uncontrollably while she supported herself with the back of a chair …

Following my grandfather's death, my parents visited Hangzhou again. My mother's half-brother Lu, who was in high school then, said, "As soon as your mother came to Hangzhou, she picked me up from the school and took me to her hotel room to take a bath."

How daunting my mother's role must have been, only in her early thirties, to be saddled with so many responsibilities: mothering six young children, looking after family and other relations, playing a gracious hostess for my father's social activities, and, most incredibly, she did all that through numerous pregnancies and births.

Despite his busy life at work and a wide social circle, my father was very involved in raising the kids. In Nanjing, my oldest brother, Long, was the only one old enough to go to school. He remembers, "Father took me to school on the first day of school, through a cobblestoned yard in front of the kindergarten."

In one of his letters to me, Uncle Jia wrote about Father as an intellectual even though he was in politics:

> He talked with much passion about his friendship with the writer Wong Li Xi. He was very proud of his collections of Chinese paintings and calligraphy by Fu Bao Shi and Shen Yin Mo …Once he came home with a couple of porcelain pieces he had found at the Temple of Confucius (the antique market in the city). He went to great lengths to explain the uniqueness of each piece …

Father had a long-standing friendship with Fu Bao Shi. It was my father who, along with several friends, organized an exhibition for Fu, and as a result, Fu's artistic standing was elevated to that of renowned masters such as Qi Bai Shi. Father had a few of Fu's paintings in our Taiwan home. I used to sneak into Father's study and stare at a scroll with an old man and his daughter playing flute in front of another lady. For me, it was as moving as Picasso's paintings during his Blue Period. Unfortunately, after father's death, as my siblings and I were all in foreign countries, some of his collections simply disappeared.

Among the guests who frequented our Nanjing house were the writer Hu Qiu Yuan and He Yangling, a cousin with whom Father started his political career. In doing research for this story, I contacted his son, Renfu, in Hangzhou. He wrote me a long letter in reply:

> In the summer of 1947, my father died unexpectedly, a total shock to my mother and us. If it weren't for your father, who arranged the funeral and sorted out other matters for us, I really can't imagine how we would have survived that shattering experience.

After the tour of the house, we traced the daily route my father took to the former Ministry of Finance, where he worked as the special advisor from 1946 to 1948. Going through the neighborhood alleyways, we met local people holding their birdcages, filling the air with messages of spring. The French plane trees on both sides of the major streets extended their bare arms to the cool breeze. "What an elegant and stately city Nanjing is," I thought. No wonder as many as six ancient Chinese dynasties made it their capital, and it is more tragic that it became the target of unprecedented Japanese atrocities in the beginning of the war (1927–1928). Through the passage of time, people lived and died as they survived against all odds and passed down enduring legacies from generation to generation. Returning to the place where my parents had spent an important part of their lives moved me to the verge of tears. I could now connect myself to the past, however tenuous it is, and appreciate what a special gift it was that I had lived with my family in a legendary place like Nanjing.

Our Home in Shanghai

In response to my inquiry about our home in Shanghai, my brother, Long, wrote me a message: "For about a year, Father took the train to Shanghai every Monday, only came home on the weekends. The rest of us didn't move to Shanghai until after our youngest brother, Duan, was born in October 1948."

It was therefore not unreasonable to assume that while the family was still in Nanjing, my father had already been living in Shanghai, working as the executive vice president of Central Trust. During that period, he also served a special commission called "Attacking Tigers" with Jiang Jing Guo, which was aimed at stopping corruption.

Through a series of inquiries, I found out that of all my parents' old friends and acquaintances, the only ones still living in Shanghai were Min-Rui and Mrs. Hao. They both stayed in our second Shanghai home after we left.

With a strong sense of urgency, I took a trip to Shanghai with my husband. Min-Rui met us at the hotel lobby, and we went straight to the house where we had lived as a family.

After taking a couple of side streets, we arrived at an alley off Tai An Road, parallel to the thoroughfare of Huai Hai Road. Following the winding alley flanked by shrubberies, we came to a cul-de-sac with four or five three-story stucco houses. Our house was the last one in the row. It had turned into a multifamily dwelling, with bicycles parked in the entranceway and laundry hanging on the balconies. Even the garage was now divided into a three-room apartment.

We found one of the residents willing to escort us on a quick tour of the house. Upon entering, we encountered a staircase. Facing it was the original dining room with a semicircular window facing the backyard. Behind the staircase was the kitchen, apparently for communal use now. On the left side of the staircase, two rooms faced the front yard. They were used as the main reception rooms when we lived there. Up toward the second floor on the middle landing of the stairs, there was a room, probably a children's nursery. On the second floor, there were three rooms: one big room facing the front yard and two smaller ones facing the back. According to Min-Rui, my parents had occupied the master bedroom with the babies, and the other two had been Cousin Ming's room and Father's study. The third floor had a similar floor plan, but as the landing was now utilized as a kitchenette, we had to stop our tour there. The third floor was used for guests when we lived there. In 1948, Father's friend, Mr. Duan Xi Peng, the leader of the May Fourth movement, stayed with us when he was seeking medical care in Shanghai.

Coming out of the house, we walked into the backyard, where the condition was no better. A few unhealthy-looking trees grew against the walls around the house, but one couldn't find a single blade of grass on the ground, let alone flowers. Junk was piled up under a shelter with green plastic roofing. The balconies from the second and third floors were full of empty boxes for appliances. Most amazingly, there was the broken WELL that I always remembered! Now, I could say for sure that I had identified the house in which we had lived. It is the house I visited now, not Madame Soong's Museum on the main thoroughfare of Huai Hai Road

When I shared this finding with my siblings, it conjured up old memories for them. My brother, Long, confirmed that it was indeed the house in which we had lived. "When our entire family moved to Shanghai, we first stayed in a big house, but only for a short while," he told me over the phone. He continued, "Mother thought it unsafe for the kids to live in a house close to the major thoroughfare. We moved as soon as the Central Trust found a suitable house for the family." The mystery of two houses was finally solved.

To me, whether the Soong Museum was once our home is not important anymore. What means the most is that, in the process of searching for our Shanghai home, I found out a piece of history that had been totally forgotten during the passage of half a century.

Father's Last Mission in Shanghai

Toward the end of 1948, the civil war with the Chinese Communist Party (CCP) intensified. After winning the decisive Xu Bang (or Huai Hai) battle in December 1948, the CCP armies pushed their way toward major cities in northern China. In the early part of the following year, Chiang Kai-shek resigned as the leader of the republic.

It was around that time my family left the mainland. Uncle Kui recalled, "It was already tough getting air tickets. That's why your family went to Taiwan by sea instead."

My oldest brother, who was seven then as the oldest of six children, remembered the trip well. "After we boarded the ship, Father took me around to visit the machine room and other cool stuff. He taught us how to eat Western-style meals in the large dining room. During the trip, the ship stopped by the coast to pick up soldiers from the Xu Bang battle. Father asked Mother to let the wounded use our cabins."

Yet, according to Cousin Mao, my father didn't go to Taiwan

with us. "Your mother and you kids went to Taiwan first," he said. "My sister, Ming, told me that in March your father took her out of the mainland by plane."

Uncle Kui echoed what Mao said, "After your mother and you children had left, I recall seeing your father in Shanghai a number of times."

Now, a half century later, Min-Rui confirmed that my father stayed in Shanghai until the eve of liberation in early May of 1949. She was the one who saw my father off at Shanghai Hongqiao airport.

Given all the information I had collected, I gathered the sequence of events were as follows: Father first took the family to Taiwan at the end of 1948. Once we were settled, he went back to Shanghai, not once but several times, right up until the eve of the Communist occupation of the city.

Why did my father risk his own life going back to Shanghai? He had an important mission to accomplish. To establish an exile government in Taiwan with a contingency of five million government functionaries, Chiang Kai-shek charged the chairman of the Chinese Central Bank, Yu Hong Jun, to transfer the government's treasury to Taiwan with logistic support from the minister of Navy, Gui Yong Qing. Father was responsible for transporting the treasury, including the gold and foreign currencies, to Taiwan.

My interview with Wong Zhi Nan in California, a former student of my father, revealed that Father had started the operation even before our family's ocean journey to Taiwan. One day Wong got the word from my father that he would pass by Keelung, the seaport in northern Taiwan. With an infant daughter in his arms, Wong saw my father descend from a Navy vessel, wearing a khaki suit and a safari hat. After a brief exchange of greetings, Father turned around to board the ship, which immediately sailed away and disappeared behind the horizon.

During his numerous trips to Shanghai, Father spared no time helping other family members and friends get out of the mainland. My mother's niece, Cousin Ming, didn't go to Taiwan with us because she was about to graduate from the university in Shanghai. In March, the university granted early diplomas to all graduating students. As promised, my father brought Ming to Taiwan safely. She lived with us as a member of the family until she got married.

In his letter to me five decades later, He Renfu, the son of my father's cousin and political mentor, recalled what had happened during that chaotic year of political uncertainty:

> In March 1949, I finished college and went to Shanghai. Your father had someone escort me to his house—your mother and you children were already gone. By that time, I had already landed a job offer in Zhejiang and opted to stay in China. This was the last time I saw your father ...Since then we have lost contact with each other in the far ends of the world.

In late April, as the CCP armies were approaching the Yangtze River, and the fall of Nanjing and Shanghai was imminent, it became increasingly difficult for my father to accomplish his mission to bring Central Trust's foreign exchange reserve to Taiwan. Most of his colleagues had either left the country or defected to the CCP armies. In that crucial moment, Father got hold of the key individual at the airport, whose signature was required to have the funds transferred to a foreign bank in Hong Kong. Mr. Lo Shi Shi, Chiang Kai-shek's wartime press secretary who was also a long-standing friend of Father, wrote an essay about this event paying tribute to my father:

> In a situation of "hanging a thousand tons with a thin thread," Mr. Ho [my father] commanded his extraordinary leadership resisting the landslide and gaining control over the foreign exchange reserve ... and at the last moment he managed to transfer the entire fund to a foreign bank, which would otherwise have fallen into the hands of the enemy ...

According to the archive, the Kuomintang (KMT) government brought $300 million worth of foreign exchange reserves to Taiwan. It may seem minuscule by today's standards (equivalent to $3.2 billion today), but it was nevertheless essential to an unprecedented population surge in Taiwan. The foreign exchange brought to Taiwan from Central Trust alone exceeded the total amount of the currency issued. Thanks to that financial infusion, the exile government was able to issue the New Taiwan currency in June, balance the budget, and control inflation, thus paving the way for Taiwan's long-term economic growth and prosperity. Documentation of this event has been made available in recent years in both Communist and KMT archives. Yet the credit was given to Yu Hong Jun, the chairman of Shanghai Central Bank of China.

Father didn't leave Shanghai until the day before the Communist armies entered the city. Min-Rui, who stayed in the house with Father along with another relative after we had left Shanghai, described the situation: "Your father said to me, 'The news has it that CCP armies are about to cross the river, as one can hear the drums beating across the river. I really cannot stay any longer.' Before he left, your father had stocked the house with all sorts of dry goods. He also gave me twenty American dollars, saying, 'Keep this for emergency use.'"

In that life-or-death moment, my father sent a letter to his most trusted brother (whom we called "Fourth Uncle") in England, the very last letter he sent from the country to which he would never return, a letter without a single word but with a photo of his six children, as if to say, these are my beloved ones; please take care of them should I perish before reaching the free world. How he must have been torn between his desire to be with his family and his strong sense of duty toward the government to which he had dedicated his life, energy, and faith! He certainly did not expect his brother would choose to return to Beijing to join the opposite side of China.

In the ensuing decades, China followed a treacherous course of political movements with many innocent lives wasted. In Taiwan, where my parents welcomed their seventh child, my family was completely cut off from any connection with the mainland. As the seasons changed, the children went from one grade to the next, wih little knowledge of what had happened in that unreachable past. Our only responsibility was to do well at school and to move up from one grade to the next. We didn't appreciate how lucky we were to have a complete family with both parents and seven siblings under one roof. I cannot imagine what would have happened if we had been left behind on the mainland.

Only a few years after settling in Taiwan, my father left his political career. In his autobiography, he wrote:

> With a blunt and direct nature, I could not help but fight against evil. Yet, I have also created many enemies. I am someone who could deal with business but not people. Even though I am often confronted with objections, the final verdict will be in my favor ...

In 1982 he died in the United States during a family visit, and we held a memorial for him in Taiwan. Jiang Jing Guo, the president of the ROC, sent a handwritten scroll commemorating his contribution to the Republic of China in exile.

With the passing of more than a half century, events have become history. Father and Mother are long gone, but their children have built their lives with dignity and prosperity in many corners of the world. In remembering our parents, we feel a profound gratitude toward them, for bringing us to this world, for raising us under very harsh circumstances, and most of all, for risking their own lives to keep us safe and give us the opportunity to live in a free world. It is the unconditional love they had for us and their spirit of compassion and commitment toward others that made their lives significant. Having revisited our childhood homes, I cherish even more the special legacy our parents left behind.

Reunion

My father married late. "My father—your grandfather—died when I was fourteen," he used to tell us. "As one of the elder sons, I shouldered the burden of the entire family." Father raised his younger brothers and sisters before getting married himself. He was a fierce brother to his siblings and a severe father to his children.

Around late 1948, as the Chinese Communists were poised to take over China, our family moved to Taiwan from the mainland with the Nationalist government. Some of my father's siblings stayed behind; there was no communication between them for as long as three decades. Growing up in Taiwan, I knew very little about my father's family. What happened in China was shrouded in mystery in my childhood world.

Years later, I came across a snapshot of a young couple in front of the London Tower Bridge in one of the family albums. The woman was wearing an elegant overcoat and a pair of high heels. The man looked handsome and distinguished in a light-colored suit. When I asked my mother who these people were, she lowered her voice. "They are Fourth Uncle and Aunt. Don't you ever mention this to anybody!" Later, I learned from relatives that one of my father's brothers had joined the Chinese Communist Party (CCP) while serving as a diplomat for the Nationalist government.

The young couple in the photo were this infamous uncle and his wife.

During the 1950s, Taiwan's government was particularly paranoid about national security regarding the mainland. Fourth Uncle's "defection" put my father in an awkward situation. One day, he was stopped by two plainclothes intelligence officers who asked him to go to the police headquarters for a "conversation." Father managed to return home unscathed, but the stigma remained and cost him dearly in politics. After that, nobody in the family ever mentioned Fourth Uncle, as if he had never existed.

Thirty years later, in the summer of 1980, when China had barely come out of its tumultuous Cultural Revolution, I received a letter from my brother in Los Angeles: "Fourth Uncle is coming to New York for a United Nations meeting. Would you be able to meet him?" Meeting this mysterious Fourth Uncle in person was something beyond my wildest dreams.

My husband and I lived in Maryland then. With some trepidation, we went to New York and met Fourth Uncle at the Chinese Mission House in Midtown Manhattan. Fourth Uncle looked radiant, youthful for sixty, somewhat slightly built in a not-so-perfectly tailored suit, typical for Chinese men of that era. Overall, he exuded confidence, apparently at ease with himself. "This is certainly not one of Father's hometown folks," I thought.

After initial exchanges of formality, he said, "My wife and I were so shocked and saddened by the news of your mother's passing. She was such a fine lady, always kind to us." My mother had died almost twenty years before.

He continued, "How is your father? I can't imagine how Second Brother would bear it."

My father had been an unhappy man in the years since Mother's passing, with frequent insomnia and unpredictable moodiness. But what could I, or what should I, say to this uncle, whom I was meeting for the first time?

"Father is fine," I replied. Yet my lips started to tremble and my voice was choked with tears.

In an armchair across from me, Fourth Uncle looked at me intently, tears glistening in his eyes. "Your father was more than a brother to me," he said. "He was the most influential figure in my life."

Fourth Uncle was the youngest sibling in my father's family of four boys and four girls. As a young adult, my father worked part-time to support his family. He gave up the opportunity to attend one of the most prestigious universities in Beijing; instead, he went to the provincial university so that he could take care of his family. Meanwhile, he was involved in local politics and was recognized by the provincial governor for his talents and potential. In 1929, my father was awarded a government scholarship to study in the United States and Great Britain. Throughout his five years abroad, he used part of his stipend to provide for his family back home. When he returned to China in 1934, he had a number of job offers. He accepted a government position in Nanjing, the capital of China at the time, as it offered the best schools in the nation. He moved the entire family with him so that his brothers and sisters could benefit from a good education.

Fourth Uncle, prodigiously bright and full of ambition, was my father's favorite sibling. Every Monday, the two of them took the train together for work and school. The two brothers always had much to discuss, despite their fifteen-year difference in age.

In July 1937 the Sino-Japanese war broke out. Upon graduation from high school, Fourth Uncle studied international law at Central University of Political Sciences in the wartime national capital of Chongqing. My father had a degree in international law himself, but his career in the government was largely administrative, something he very much regretted. Yet Father spared nothing in promoting his brother's career in the foreign service. In 1944, when Fourth Uncle got married in Chongqing, Father addressed the wedding banquet: "It is my most ardent wish that my brother continues my unfulfilled career."

Fourth Uncle had met his wife in the foreign ministry training program specifically designed for young diplomats. Nine years older than Fourth Uncle, Fourth Aunt had two sons from a previous marriage. In that era, it was simply unthinkable for a young man like Fourth Uncle to fall head over heels in love with a woman like her. Even when we met him a half-century later, Fourth Uncle still raved about his wife's "unmatched beauty and poise." Father was liberal enough not to oppose their marriage, but he certainly did not expect that his brother would marry someone who worked underground for the CCP. Soon after the wedding, Fourth Uncle, along with his wife, went to London as the deputy consul for the Chinese embassy under the Nationalist government. At the same time, he was working on a PhD in England.

In late 1948, as the CCP victory was within reach, Fourth Aunt returned to China alone. Fourth Uncle, having just finished his PhD, followed her to Beijing when the CCP proclaimed the People's Republic of China in the following year.

Upon Fourth Uncle's "defection" to the Communists, all communications between the brothers were severed. "We are only three brothers," my father said to his other two brothers. "Why do you count him as your brother?" I can't imagine the shock, rage, and dismay my father must have felt at that moment.

Thirty years later, following the United States' recognition of Communist China, other nations around the world, one after another, established diplomatic ties with China. The situation between Taiwan and China changed completely. It was at that juncture that Fourth Uncle started his career with the United Nations.

After our first meeting in New York, every time Fourth Uncle came to the United Nations, he also took a trip to visit us in Maryland. We anticipated his visits with as much excitement as if he were our own parent. At the same time, he arranged for my husband and myself to give lectures in China. Father in Taiwan also learned from us about what had become of Fourth Uncle. Though he still expressed strong distaste for the Communists—"Having fought against them all my life, I would never trust any of them," he said—he didn't seem to mind the idea of meeting Fourth Uncle when we suggested it.

In early 1982, Father visited us in Maryland while Fourth Uncle was in New York for a UN meeting. As usual, he came to Washington, DC, after his official duties were complete.

When the weekend came, my husband and I went to the Chinese embassy in the city to pick up Fourth Uncle while Father stayed at our house. As soon as we pulled the car into the driveway with Uncle in the back seat, Father, still in his slippers, rushed out of the house to greet us. When we stopped the car and let Fourth Uncle out, he called, "Second Brother!"

"Fourth Brother," my father replied. Two pairs of hands were locked together instantly.

Between 1944, when Fourth Uncle left China for England, and 1982, when the brothers met again, many changes had occurred: Father had left the Nationalist political arena long before and was leading a simple life teaching at the universities. As for Fourth Uncle and his wife, they did not fare very well in China either, as intellectuals with a foreign education. During the Cultural Revolution, they were sent to labor camps in the countryside of Hunan province. Fourth Aunt's older son was jailed for many years. Her younger son killed himself by jumping out of his apartment. She herself suffered from a nervous breakdown from which she never fully recovered.

Throughout that day, the brothers talked mostly about what had happened to their family members. Although I could only understand part of their conversation in Jiangxi dialect, it was obvious that Father's personal concern for his family far outweighed their political differences. Fourth Uncle didn't utter a word about the hardships he had endured under the Communist regime. On the contrary, he expressed gratitude for his wife: "If it weren't for her, I wouldn't be here to represent China in the United Nations." Father didn't blame Fourth Uncle or his wife but expressed the regret that they didn't have any children who would carry on Fourth Uncle's many talents.

On the way as we took him back to the embassy later that day, Fourth Uncle said to me, "Your father is 'my brother, my father, my teacher' (亦兄, 亦父, 亦師)." When I relayed this message to Father, he nodded his head and sighed deeply. All was forgiven.

From his first mission to the United Nations until his official retirement in 2002, Fourth Uncle reached the pinnacle of his career as the commissioner to the UN International Law Commission for four consecutive terms, representing 1.4 billion Chinese people. Fourth Uncle indeed lived up to the highest expectations any brother, father, or teacher could have.

Only a few months after that meeting in Maryland, Father had a stroke while in Los Angeles, which rendered him immobile and speechless. When one of Father's hometown friends visited him in the hospital, tears welled up in his eyes. How he must have longed for his beloved family in his homeland!

> He faded away, sorrowfully left
> alone in a faraway land
> where the Yellow Plum[1] Rain pours to no end.
> Great talents unfulfilled, as a noble
> bird born in a rough world,
> suddenly awakened from a
> dream and bid farewell.

---

[1] . Yellow Plum symbolizes the spring. My father died in May of that year.

Mother's Illness

I was a worry-free kid growing up in Taiwan ... until my mother fell ill.

When I was about thirteen, we started to have breakfast taken out from the breakfast stalls on the street corner, and the New Year's Eve feast became a potluck dinner. All I knew was that Mother was too tired to do it. We didn't know she had cancer; Father hid the dismal truth from everyone, including the patient herself.

For a while, Mother went in and out of the hospital for treatment, sometimes overnight. Later, Father had a hospital bed installed in the house so she could receive treatments at home. One day I noticed her palms were unusually smooth, free of the lines etched by years of household chores. She reacted to my discovery rather optimistically, saying, "I have worked hard with my hands all these years. It must be the Good Heaven who wants me to take a break."

I didn't worry too much about it either, believing she would recover from this health issue as she had from other kinds of afflictions. In fact, she managed to recover from her illness once, but only briefly. I noticed her back was bent slightly after prolonged bed rest, and her hair became coarse and frazzled without its usual luster.

One day, while Father was out, Big Uncle stopped by and left a note. When Father read the note, he went into a thunderous rage, so angry that he threw a whole set of keys onto the floor and made a dent in it. I didn't know what made him so angry until many years later, when we found the note in one of Father's desk drawers. It said: "I understand your wife's illness is incurable. Don't be overwhelmed by grief, my brother. It is about time to face the eventuality and prepare for the necessary afterlife logistics." Father was determined to help Mother fight against all odds, but it was a hefty load for him to carry it all on his own.

During the final year of her illness, Mother stayed in the hospital almost all the time. I was in the eleventh grade. On my way home from school, I would usually stop by the hospital to visit her. Every time I entered the dim hospital room, Mother's eyes would light up. She would answer my greetings and listen quietly to my chatter. With a great effort, she would urge me to go home before it turned dark. I pulled my jacket tightly around myself and dashed out into the chilliness of early spring.

Just before the next school year began, the school organized a one-week field trip to the south of Taiwan for the senior class. When I asked Father to sign the parental consent, he appeared very reluctant. "Your Ma is very sick; do you have to go that far?"

"But everyone is going, Papa, this is the chance of a lifetime!"

As soon as we boarded the train, amid commotion and excitement, I felt uneasy. The words— "Your Ma is very sick"— rang in my ears, over and over, and in such a grave tone. "Your Ma is very sick; do you have to go that far?" How I wished the train would turn around and take me back. After a miserable long week, I boarded the train back to Taipei. As soon as it pulled into the station, I quickly headed for the hospital without saying goodbye to my friends. I took a shortcut on the muddy paths crisscrossing the rice fields. In the pitch darkness, the warm air was filled with the sounds of frogs croaking and insects humming.

When I reached the hospital, the familiar lobby suddenly looked disproportionately large and empty. I started to run through door after door, corridor after corridor, and finally arrived at Mother's room. The door was half shut; all was quiet. Trying to catch my breath, I was suddenly seized by a sinking feeling. Is she still there? What if something happened to her while I was away? After much hesitation, in a trembling voice I whispered, "M— ... Ma ..." I couldn't believe it when I heard her faint reply from the dark recess of the room! "She is all right, I was being silly," I said to myself and walked in.

Summer soon waned into autumn. Every time I saw Mother, she would remind me to wear a jacket. She was most upset when I showed her the injuries on my knees caused by a bike incident and urged me to have a proper nurse take care of them. To this day, every time I touch the scar on my knee, I remember my mother in her hospital bed, with her tenderness and endless worries about her children.

Then it happened.

On a perfectly clear autumn morning when class was in session, I heard my name announced on the loudspeaker. I knew right then, the moment I had dreaded for so long had come. I tossed all my stuff into my bag and rushed downstairs to the school reception room. Everyone turned silent when I entered. Father's former chauffeur was waiting for me. My heart sank. Father has not had a chauffeured car for many years; why is he here? I got into the car. When I saw my younger brothers and sister, I burst into uncontrollable sobs.

In the hospital room, my father and my older brothers and sister were waiting. Five or six people from Father's former office were standing in the antechamber. I avoided their pitying expressions and walked straight toward my mother's bed. Her eyes were shut tightly, and she couldn't speak, but I noticed her hands moving slightly, almost imperceptibly, as if she were trying to touch her boys and girls on both sides of her. A missionary lady came, whispering prayers in her ear. Tiny teardrops escaped from the corners of her eyes, slowly moving past her temples toward her ears. No one uttered a sound except for the doctors, who whispered as they moved in and out of the room like shadows. Time seemed to stand still. When the clock above the bed struck midnight, one of the doctors pronounced the patient dead, and he pulled up a blanket from the end of the bed to cover her body. It was November 1, 1960. Mother was forty-four years old. She left behind her seven children; the oldest was nineteen and the youngest was less than ten.

I don't know how I spent the next few days. The house was full of people. I heard one of my little brothers weeping. I felt utterly lonely and empty. The world was simply incomprehensible. When I returned to school, I said nothing to my friends about my mother, nor did any of them ask about her. Overnight the world was divided into two: one part belonged to those who still had their parents, and the other to those who had lost one or both.

Journey to the Sea

I met your father in Boston in the summer of 1967 when I visited the US from Europe. I was twenty-two, he was twenty-eight. I got in touch with him through his brother, whom I had met a year earlier. I called him before the trip, and he sounded reserved: "Yes, my brother requested that I pick you up at the airport." He came with a 1957 sky-blue Chevrolet that had a prominent pair of wings at the tail. A bit short, merely an inch or two taller than I, wearing a pair of baggy pants, half nerdy and half shy, that was how he appeared to me in our first encounter. The moment he cast his first glance at me he was smitten, as if meeting someone who would make him the happiest, and perhaps the most miserable, person in the world. How did I know that? I don't know, but I'm sure of that even to this day.

We hit it off right away. It took no time for us to find out we had a great deal in common: both of us had graduated from Taiwan University, and our families were among the millions who had migrated to Taiwan from mainland China following the Nationalist government. From day one he became a fixed part of my daily routines. Every morning I woke up to his call outside the rooming house where I was staying: "The sun is up now; I have been waiting here since dawn."

We spent the summer together. What a splendid summer it

was, basking in the warm New England sun, watching Frisbees flying on the banks of the Charles River. The flow of life and joy, the summer of our youth, hair flowing in the breeze, eyes searching for the stars in the night sky.

We were inseparable. Cooking on a century-old stove in his basement apartment, savoring ice cream cones from Howard Johnson's at Harvard Square, whispering in the libraries, admiring world-class treasures in the museums, making fun of our own shadows in the water while counting the "Smoot" (a non-standard humorous unit of length created as a MIT fraternity prank) across Harvard Bridge. Above all, we shared our dreams, plans, and stories.

Of all the events in his early life, I was most impressed by his journey out of China. "Do you know how my family came out of the mainland? My mother took me, my sister, and an au pair girl to the southern border of China. There, we crawled through a tunnel underneath the barbed wire to reach Hong Kong."

Here he is, a Harvard student working on his PhD all the way from underneath the barbed wire in southern China to Cambridge, Massachusetts in the United States. How unbelievable! But I knew it was a true story as soon as I met his eyes, intense and sincere behind a pair of dark-rimmed glasses.

He went on saying, "On the eve before the Communist forces arrived at Chengdu (in Sichuan province), my family was prepared to take a flight to Taiwan. After a torturously long wait at the airport, and amid confusion and chaos, my father and my older brother got on the last flight out of Chengdu; the rest of us returned to the city. It was not until a year later that we were reunited with my father and brother in Taiwan."

Your paternal grandfather, Cheng Ti-Xuan (whom you called "Ye Ye"), was a scholar in Chinese classics, best known for his poetry work in the genre of Chuci. Do you still remember his study in the attic of their house in Taipei? Your dad often reminisced that his father read and wrote in his study all day long and the sound of his reciting poems would reverberate all over the neighborhood.

From what your dad said about his mother, I came to know Nai Nai as a remarkable mother even before I met her in person many years later. A woman with all the traditional feminine virtues, she was extraordinarily resolved and resilient. If Ye Ye was the icon for the children, Nai Nai was the guardian angel of the family.

Ye Ye worked for the Examination Bureau, a government body that administered civil services. He also taught in colleges as a scholar in Chuci. "What's unique about my father's poems is that they reflect the modern life and spirit in an elegant literary form," your dad said.

To piece together this story, I dug into Cheng Ti-Xuan's numerous collections of poems and found a great deal of information surrounding the circumstances under which your father escaped from the mainland.

It is a story about a family's escape from China. It is also a story about how the family survived a treacherous journey in pursuit of a promising future. This story epitomizes the sorrow of an entire generation of Chinese, and hopefully it will bring hope and aspiration to future generations.

∾

Ye Ye and Nai Nai had seven children. In Taiwan, your dad only had an older brother and a younger sister; the rest of his siblings had perished in China. Two never survived infancy, one sister died of illness during the civil war (1946–1949), one brother, who had been adopted by a childless uncle when your dad was born, died during the Cultural Revolution (1966–1976).

As a civil servant, Ye Ye, along with his family, followed the government wherever it went. At the end of 1948, after winning the Battle of Huaihai, the Chinese Communist armies were poised to take over the northern half of the country. Chiang Kai-shek resigned as the head of state, and the new leader, Li Zong Ren, proceeded to establish a separate government in southern China vis-a-vis the Communist government in the north. As a result, many Nationalist government units were migrating en masse from eastern cities to the southern provinces of Guangdong, Guangxi, and Sichuan, as dictated by the fluid political situation. Those travels were extremely difficult for families with children.

"For a while we stayed in Wuzhou in Guangxi province," your dad told me. "It's at this juncture that one of my younger sisters got very sick with a high fever."

Each year during the flood season, Wuzhou, which is situated on the River Xi, was inundated with water that could reach as high as twenty feet. That was the situation when his family was in Wuzhou, camping out in a schoolhouse, separated from other families only by sheets hung on clotheslines. With torrents of water roaring outside and all means of transportation cut off, the parents could only watch the sister's fever run its course. "When my sister died, my father sat alone in the darkness crying. He cried for the tragic fate of his family, he cried for the untimely death of my sister, he cried for the turmoil endured by the nation." How horrified your dad must have felt, and how sad it was for a child to learn the tragic fate of human beings so early in life!

In an elegy for his daughter, Ye Ye wrote, "My poor child! You are not old enough to know the local dialect. Leaving you behind, my sorrows hurt deeper." But the family had no choice. As soon as the flood waters receded, they buried the girl and kept going with the exodus to Sichuan province.

In the ensuing months, the family settled in Chengdu, where Ye Ye found a teaching position at a local college, hoping the negotiation with the Communists would allow the Nationalist government to keep part of the country. However, the Communist forces, after taking over the eastern part of China, kept advancing unabated toward the major cities in the southwest.

After what seemed a short span of normal life in Chengdu, the family had to travel again, this time to the last fortress of Taiwan. To reach the airport, the transport car took them over mountain roads, zigzagging among the rice paddies on step-like terraces. It would have been a lovely excursion for the kids if it hadn't been for the war.

When they finally arrived at the airport, rumors about the Communist troops approaching the city were spreading like wildfire. In every corner of the waiting area, masses of humanity congregated, luggage piled in heaps, while gangs of rascals cajoled people into illegal trading of household items. Realizing that the worst was yet to come, Ye Ye and Nai Nai came up with a plan for the likelihood of being separated from each other. She would take the younger kids back to Chengdu, and he would go ahead with the oldest boy, your dad's older brother, to Taiwan. After what seemed like forever, a plane bearing the Nationalist logo broke through the thick clouds in an overcast sky and landed on the tarmac like a giant silver bird. With no time to waste, one of Ye Ye's students, holding two tickets in his hand, pushed Ye Ye and the oldest son through densely packed crowds toward the entrance gate. The door shut just as the last two passengers entered. Then the plane took off and soon disappeared into the thick clouds from which it had come. Here went the last flight out of Chengdu to Taiwan.

Left alone with two young children and a teenage girl in Chengdu, Nai Nai managed to find housing with a relative in the city. Meanwhile, she decided to travel to Wuhan (in Hebei province) over 1,200 kilometers away, where she would join her brother's family and wait for news from Ye Ye, who was now in Taiwan with their oldest son.

The journey from Chengdu to Chongqing, then to Wuhan proved to be more than just treacherous; it was hair-raising. The great poet Li Bai (701–762) wrote, "The difficulty of the Shu (ancient name for Sichuan) Road is more difficult than going to the blue sky." The transport vehicles, with people sitting on top of the canvas, took narrow paths through deep mountain gorges, followed closely by Communist army convoys. From time to time, the sound of falling rocks echoed hauntingly in the ravines hundreds of feet below. Your dad still recalled, "Once, as soon as we crossed a bridge, a big explosion shook the ground. When I turned around, everything behind us was shrouded in a huge cloud of dust—the bridge had been blown to pieces, and all the vehicles beyond it halted."

Once the mother and children were settled in Wuhan, she sent her son to a local school. "I enjoyed going to school, where l learned the drum dance, the symbol of the peasant revolution. One day when class was in session, my mother sent a domestic helper to fetch me from school, but I refused to leave. Eventually, Mother came to school herself and dragged me home."

Your dad could be quite stubborn, even as a child. Nai Nai loved to tell this story about him: "As a toddler, he would eat by himself in a highchair. But if I gave him too much, he would toss the bowl on the floor; if there was too little, he would do the same. Everything must be just right for him."

Meanwhile, Ye Ye in Taiwan had arranged for the family to get out of mainland China via Hong Kong. The timing was essential, as China in 1950 still maintained a border link with Hong Kong.

With an escort, the mother and three kids took the train to Guangzhou in the south. It was an eye-opening experience for a child with a growing mind. Scene after scene flying past the windows, crossing the mile-long Yangtze Bridge, racing from the dark, cold, and muddy Hubei to mountainous Hunan, then the ubiquitous rice paddies of southern China. After arriving at

Guangzhou, in the balmy air of the city, they boarded a commuter train for what is known as Shenzhen today but was only a piece of wasteland bordering Hong Kong's New Territories in the 1950s.

In crossing the border, the mother, with all her valuables sewn inside the quilt she was wearing, hired a "yellow cow" (smuggler) to lead them through the tunnel under the barbed wire. Walking on halfway-bound feet—her feet had been bound as a child, a relic of a custom practiced by affluent families—the mother, along with three children, miraculously made it through the most crucial passage of their journey.

When they emerged on the other side of the tunnel, they were caught by a policeman in a British uniform. That meant they could be sent back to China. Without hesitation, the mother handed the man a piece of gold. That was how the family finally reached the free world.

Unfortunately, his mother's brother in Wuhan, who had been the mayor of a small township and was also a small landowner, was executed under the pretext of collaboration with the Nationalists.

His mother's greatest regret was that she couldn't reach her second son in the countryside, who had been adopted in infancy by an uncle. For years, she never ceased to look for her lost child, and eventually she found out that he had died of a postoperative complication during the Cultural Revolution.

※

In the 1960s and '70s, the common path for a young person who completed his or her college education in Taiwan was to go abroad for graduate studies. Upon graduation from Taiwan University, your father applied to graduate school at Harvard and was accepted. "When I left Taiwan, my father accompanied me to Keelung (one of the deep-water harbors in Taiwan) to see me off. Once on board the ship, I looked back and saw my father weeping, and that image has remained in me all these years away from home."

In pursuing his PhD at Harvard, your dad chose astronomy as his major. When we first met, he took me to the historical Harvard-Smithsonian observatory on Concord Avenue. His enthusiasm for astronomy was apparent when he described his vision of the solar system, his eyes wide open as if seeing a miracle unfolding in front of him. "Is that why you chose astronomy instead of a more practical branch of physics?" I asked him.

"I have always dreamed of being an explorer, exploring places like the North Pole and the Antarctic. Astronomy, by definition, is exploring the universe. It suits me well," he said.

Then he added, "On my voyage to the States, I watched the sunrise and sunset over the horizon while ships moved in and out of sight. I loved the sensation of waves rocking underneath the deck; I never suffered from seasickness like other passengers. You can't imagine how amazing and surreal it is to be surrounded by celestial bodies in total darkness and silence. I have since bonded with the sea, so much so that I named myself Hai (Sea) for my alternate name."

Above all, he found in me the person with whom he wanted to share the journey of his life.

We got married in Harvard Yard a year later, only two weeks after I had returned from Europe. We managed to rent an apartment, and we bought a bridal gown and a veil for me, a two-piece suit for him, and a ring with our initials and the wedding date on it. As far as I can remember, your dad never wore the ring. As simple as our wedding was, we hired an organist to play Handel's "Water Music" as I walked down the aisle on my brother's arm, nervous and excited, watched by my sister, brother-in-law, and a handful of friends from Harvard. Outside Appleton Chapel, birds chirped merrily, tender leaves were budding on the trees, and a gentle June sun danced on our smiling faces, all signifying a bright start for a new life.

The first milestone of our journey together was for him to complete his degree. We sold the Chevrolet, not without some regret, as he said, "it will soon be a prized antique car." We moved to a freshly remodeled apartment within walking distance of the observatory, a place where he had spent numerous hours dreaming and thinking. He told me about his encounter with Carl Sagan when Sagan was a lecturer there a few years before. They debated about cosmology and planned to collaborate with each other.

Working day in and day out, mornings and evenings, often with me by his side, only coming back to our little nest for meals and rest, he finally reached the end of the long road: the big day of his thesis defense. He left home in the morning and returned with a smile. A new milestone had been achieved. Interestingly, on the panel reviewing his thesis was a young man in a wheelchair named Stephen Hawking.

Now came the real challenge: finding a job. His graduate stipend from the Smithsonian was ample for two students, but not when a baby was on the way. Yes, a real human being, born from two humans, how very amazing and unthinkable! For people who had never experienced life outside of our own small world, we believed everything would work out in the end, no matter how hard—at least, that was what we wanted to believe.

He had two choices when entering the real world: going to a business as an R & D scientist or working for a pure research institute, like a government agency or a university. Single-mindedly, the young scientist in him opted for the academic path. With an acceptance letter for a postdoctoral position at NASA's Goddard Space Flight Center and a few suitcases, we boarded the train to Maryland.

As always, the unexpected happens when one is least prepared. Just before your dad was to report to work, I went into labor, and he learned that there was an issue with his job. Due to his visa status, NASA was unable to grant him the promised position—a regulation had just been enacted to prohibit federal agencies from hiring foreign nationals. To solve the dilemma, an arrangement was made so that he would be paid by the University of Maryland while working at NASA.

What should we do, and what could we do? The boat was already out of harbor, it was too late for us to turn back. Even if we did, where could we land? So, we kept on our journey down the river, hoping to reach the destination somehow, someday. Adding to the disappointment, fears of the unknown and isolation in a new city greatly dampened my adventuresome spirit and made him sick with worry. That was the real world we had to face.

In the ensuing years, as we established ourselves in Maryland, he worked initially at the University of Maryland and thereafter he was on Ball Brothers' payroll, arranged by NASA. Not having a permanent position was a chief source of discontent that often made him moody. It was also something he was too embarrassed to admit but not audacious enough to change.

When we became US citizens in 1977, he was hired by the Naval Research Laboratory in Washington, DC. For him, this was a secure path leading to what he had always wanted to be: a research scientist, particularly in the theoretical domain of astrophysics. It allowed him to explore what he had aspired to do. It also required an abundance of creative energy and a strong will to succeed. Night after night, he would toss and turn in bed, between agony and ecstasy, toying with new ideas and discoveries. In under two decades, he published over one hundred scientific papers, most of which he single-authored. Your father indeed lived up to his own aspirations.

Life went on as the world rotated around the sun, the moon around the Earth, unfeelingly and endlessly, ferocious waves pounded the sand but retreated to the ocean as limp as foam. Year after year, trees grew taller, young leaves came out, and flowers bloomed. Then a winter storm came that covered all and prostrated most. Some thrived, some perished. Neighborhoods changed, people moved in and out, houses felt smaller as the occupants transformed from crawling, to toddling, to walking, running, bicycling, and driving.

We led a typical life, working during the day, producing and publishing, and dreaming at night, when true happiness and sorrow returned. We could burst into hysterical laughter at a silly joke or into uncontrollable rage over a split decision. We deeply grieved the most tragic episode of our life, the loss of a child. More than ever since the night in Wuzhou some thirty years earlier when his sister died, your father was crushed by the tragedy of human destiny. Yet, despite everything, we hung on tightly to what we still had, hoping for a better future.

Our quest for beauty and eternity never ceased. A yearning for a big open sky and cultural inspiration always kept us going. Even during your infancy, we traveled to faraway places as a family. We were awed by the wonders inside the earth at Yellowstone, the running lava from the volcano on the Big Island, and the majestic Rocky Mountains against a cloudless sky. We were also delighted by the sight of intimate coves along the Maine coast and the busy world of small creatures in the Big Meadows at Shenandoah.

༄

As China opened its doors to the world in the early 1980s, the scope of our life suddenly took on a new dimension: the homeland we had left behind. Your dad was very excited about China's emergence on the world stage, even though it was only in a nascent state. Ever since Nixon's visit to China in 1972, he had followed the political developments closely, including the ping-pong diplomacy and the recognition of China by the United Nations. For him, science had no borders. Having collaborated with many scientists outside the US whom he had met at international conferences, he had made acquaintances with a few from China and Taiwan, and he felt quite at ease communicating with them.

Then an opportunity came. You must remember my uncle from Beijing, whom you called "Shu Gonggong," who was the diplomat representing China at the UN. He arranged for the Chinese Academy of Sciences to invite your dad to give lectures in Beijing, Xian, and Kunming in 1983. That was the beginning of what turned out to be a long-standing collaboration between Dr. CC Cheng, the Harvard-educated scientist, and the Chinese astrophysicists.

In the first couple of decades after China emerged from the disastrous Cultural Revolution, scientific research was far from meeting international standards. Those dedicated to science were constrained by their limited intellectual exposure and material resources. Your father worked with his Chinese counterparts to help them improve the quality of their research, and to share his professional expertise. He felt comfortable and close to them, perhaps because they shared a common cultural background and similar temperament. To the Chinese, he was not only highly respected but also modest and easy to work with. Dr. Wu, a good friend of your dad, used to say, "Your husband is very generous in sharing credit with those who collaborates with him." The true scientist in your father found a higher purpose that he had never had before. He had finally come home to where he belonged.

All those years that your dad worked with the Chinese scientists, we traveled with them around China. I cannot begin to tell you how I felt going back to the place we had always considered our homeland. Early one morning in 1993, when we were sailing on a passenger ship down the Yangtze River, your dad woke me up and said, "Look! We are sailing through the narrowest passage in the Three Gorges, I can even touch the cliffs." In 1994, the year before he was diagnosed with cancer, we traveled to the Silk Road with Chinese scientists, mesmerized by a peaceful and heavenly world in the oases, and privileged to read the scripts on the frescos in the Dun Huang grottos, a World Heritage site. Those trips not only left me with enduring memories, but they were also truly the highlights of our twenty-seven-year marriage.

Your dad had come home to where his dedication and labor were recognized and honored. He was named the first foreign professor by the Beijing Observatory of the Chinese Academy and one of the founding members of the Academia Sinica Institute of Astronomy and Astrophysics in Taiwan.

During his final hours at Georgetown University Hospital, he urged me to send a letter to the director of Anhui University of Technology, who had invited him for a series of lectures. He asked his host to reschedule his lectures to a later date. He wanted to continue making an impact on his home country. He wanted to dedicate himself to the place that had nourished his heart and soul.

His journey was tragically short, yet it ended in a full cycle.

Two Rochelles

March 2020

The television is blaring the news about an imminent global pandemic; the governor of New York announces that he has designated New Rochelle, a suburb of New York City, as the "COVID-19 containment center" for the area.

New Rochelle? Where is it? Why does it sound so familiar? Have I been there before? So many places have faded from memory, why does this one stand out? Perhaps it's just one of the stations along Amtrak's Northeast Corridor where I used to travel when I lived in Maryland. No, it is more significant than that.

The memories began returning to her, one after the other. Yes, she was in La Rochelle, France, during the 1968 Paris student movement. Several decades later, she drove by New Rochelle, New York every Monday when she worked on a consulting assignment with the James River paper company.

May-June 1968

Another night of student demonstrations! She looked outside the window, cobblestones on Boulevard St. Michel had been dug out and turned into a barricade to protest the Vietnam War. Naturally, the French felt strongly about the American involvement in a former French colony. The whole city was under siege and cut off from the rest of the country. Unable to concentrate on studying, she spent most of the day sending news to her fiancé in the States. "The classes are canceled again, not unexpectedly though I couldn't sleep at all. Through the night, hordes of students shouted at the police, 'Cochons, cochons,' right in front of our dorm," she wrote. "I won't be surprised if they return tonight for another big showdown."

She was engaged to a Harvard graduate student whom she had met in Cambridge the summer before. At the end of summer, she returned to Paris to work on a graduate degree in comparative literature at the Sorbonne. But what occupied the minds of the young couple that consumed most of their energy was not their respective studies but counting down the days until they could see each other again. He had managed to come to Paris during the Christmas break, quite a feat for a student during an era when air travel was not easily affordable. Yet being away from each other after the vacation proved even harder. They cried in each other's arms before his departure. She agreed to come to the States as soon as the semester ended.

The days were long for a foreign student. Her steps echoed eerily in the empty corridor of the Sorbonne. Nobody was around to answer questions; the shops and cafés were closed. *I feel so trapped here. Should I go to the States now or wait until the situation changes?* As the strike went on with no sign of abatement, she made a plan with two girlfriends to hitchhike to Bordeaux via Normandy and Brittany. In that era, hitchhiking was trendy among students. Not knowing the risks involved, like a young calf not afraid of the tiger, the three young women had a good time riding with strangers—a nagging mother and her rebellious daughter, a truck driver with a full load of Roquefort cheese, a man with a baby crib in the backseat who tried to pinch their butts. "After all, we are out of the chaotic scene in the city, how refreshing!"

They stopped by Saint-Malo, where the writer Chateaubriand was buried standing up, and then Mont Saint-Michel, the legendary medieval castle, which surfaced as the tides receded, and arrived at La Rochelle for the night. Since the food couldn't be shipped out and thus must be consumed locally, the girls enjoyed a most sumptuous feast by the sea, one they felt sure they would never forget as long as they lived.

Once back in Paris, she was beset with anxiety and fear as the city continued deteriorating. The situation in France at that time was like what she is now experiencing due to the threat of the imminent pandemic: the whole country was at a standstill, with no end in sight. I want to go home but where is my home? Not Taiwan, which she had left a couple of years earlier. Was it in the States, where she and her fiancé planned to live? What would I leave behind if I went to the States? What about my dreams, my aspirations, my opportunities, and my independence? I would never regain the sensation of culture shock seeing Paris for the first time from a bench in Tuileries Gardens. I would never have the chance to hear Professor Adam speak about Ronsard in a packed amphitheater. I would have to give up the beautiful language I so painstakingly learned and become fluent in another foreign language.

Perhaps because she couldn't resist the pressure from her fiancé, or she didn't want to risk missing the window of opportunity to escape a potential revolution, as soon as her visa for the US was granted, she got ready to leave Paris. At the news of her departure, the director of her dorm got so upset that she angrily accused everyone who left at that "crucial juncture in history" of being traitors. Her roommate, Claire, a sweet girl from Rouen, offered to take her to the airport in her Deux Chevaux. What a precious rapport she had developed in this world! She would never experience the pleasure of eating typical French food every day in the dining hall of the dorm; she would never giggle with Claire and her friend Chantal about their *petits amis*.

On their way to the airport, the news of Robert Kennedy's assassination came over the radio. The world is not safe wherever you go. I need to go where someone is always there for me. Together, we will build a place we can go home to. Within two weeks of her arrival in the States, the couple got married at the Appleton Chapel in Harvard Yard.

March 1995-December 1996

She was driving alone and couldn't figure out where she was. Why is it so dark?

A policeman stopped her car. "Ma'am, you are driving without headlights. Please show your license."

"I'm sorry, Officer ... but my husband just died. I'm completely lost."

"Oh, I'm so sorry, Ma'am." The policeman handed back her license. "You are only a few blocks from your home."

Her husband passed away in 1995 at the age of fifty-six. Upon his death, she resigned from her international assignments with Price Waterhouse. With their children away at college, the family home she and her husband had built suddenly became an empty house. He had always been there holding down the fort, whether she was away for an overseas job or working locally. He would take her to her office on his way to work and would pick her up when she was ready to wrap up the day. He would carry on with daily routines when she was away. Their son often commented, "Daddy doesn't make fancy dishes, but he always cleans up the place after cooking," knowing how his mom loved to spread ingredients and utensils all over the kitchen counter. As the husband and the father, he always monopolized the driving when the family took long vacations. They would go as far as six hundred miles a day visiting natural wonders in the Rocky Mountains, Yellowstone, and many other spectacular sights. She would never forget the Christmas Eve when she collapsed on the bathroom floor because of excessive bleeding. He was the one who followed the ambulance to the hospital and insisted on contacting a specialist to treat his wife. As a result, she had a proper hysterectomy, and her life was saved.

Living in isolation now, she felt she was floating aimlessly, like a leaf in a dark open sea. For a while she couldn't help but immerse herself in regrets and denials. How can I go on when an integral part of my life has ended? Why did I always lash out at him for dominating my life? Why couldn't I consider it a privilege to have a companion who cared about every aspect of my life? How inconsiderate and cruel I was when I went to New York with a Chinese delegation and failed to inform him of my safe arrival, which worried him to near insanity! If it weren't for the need to get the children through college, she would have had no incentive to pick up the pieces.

After a hiatus of several months from work, she found a job with a growing consulting firm. Her first assignment was with the James River Corporation in Norwalk, Connecticut. Every Monday she took an early flight from DC to LaGuardia, picked up a rental car, and went straight to the client site. New Rochelle was one of the towns she passed en route. She had no time to reflect on what the name New Rochelle signified or wonder what would have happened if she had stayed in France some twenty-eight years before; she simply drove on. For the entire week, she stayed in a hotel in nearby Stamford and did not return home until Friday afternoon. She carried on with that routine week after week. She knew it was only a job with a steady income. Nonetheless, her renewed professional status greatly helped restore her confidence and boost her outlook for the future, and most importantly, it brought her back to the hustle and bustle of the world around her. She was too occupied to cope with the pressures that came with a demanding job and to face the challenges of single parenthood. She just had to be strong and positive to survive. She just had to be forward-thinking to thrive. A silent transformation took place, and a powerful one indeed.

In the winter of 1996, her daughter, Shing started medical school at UCSF after graduating from Harvard, and her son, Ien was graduating from MIT, where he would continue to pursue a master's degree. What a stark contrast to where things had been eighteen months earlier when her husband had passed away!

For the week between Christmas and New Year's, she planned to work on the project in Connecticut; she needed billable hours to generate revenue for her firm during the holiday season. Since the project site is so close to New York City, why don't we go there for a break? The family had visited the city a couple of times before to see Broadway shows and visit the Empire State Building and the Statue of Liberty. But this is different. She had a romantic notion about New York. How fun it would be to skate on the frozen pond in Central Park and count down to the New Year at Times Square.

So, she made the plans: her daughter would stay with her at the Hyatt in Stamford during her "working vacation" while her son went to a winter camp on the West Coast with his friends. On December 31, the mother and daughter took the commuter train to Grand Central Station. As they came up from underground, Shing's boyfriend, John, was waiting, well-built and standing tall, with his usual enigmatic smile.

Shing and John had been dating since they were teenagers at fourteen and sixteen. They endured a long romantic trajectory, including many years in different colleges and medical schools. This New York adventure was part of their holiday plans.

The city felt wintry but not bitterly cold. They walked to the Waldorf-Astoria to meet up with Shing's high school friend who was working for the grand hotel. Like a bunch of country bumpkins, they marveled at the legendary building, awed by the splendid marble columns and glitzy chandeliers, delighted by the toy trains moving through a snow-clad landscape dotted with miniature Bavarian gingerbread houses.

During her years working on international assignments, she had been to most of the countries in Western Europe. When she started signing up for overseas assignments, her husband had been understandably uneasy about it. But she said, "All those years you traveled the world for scientific conferences while I stayed home with the kids. Don't you remember that I gave up everything, including my studies in France, to marry you? It's my turn to do it now." Yet, it was not the same when she traveled on business and visited the sights with her colleagues. What pleasure could there be if one wasn't sharing special experiences with loved ones? Just look how happy and radiant she was in front of a miniature Bavarian village, in the company of her family!

She can't recall how they spent the rest of the evening before the magic moment of midnight. They must have walked from one block to another. They passed by the outdoor skating rink, delighted by the sight of skaters gliding gracefully under a gray sky. It reminded her of a movie she had watched as a young girl about a man meeting a young girl by the frozen pond in Central Park. Each time he saw her, she seemed to have grown, and so did the friendship between the man and the girl as the story went on. Eventually, the girl disappeared, and the man found out she was one of the victims of the Titanic, which had sunk to the bottom of the ocean that year. So that was her notion of Central Park: tragic but magical.

After their New Year's Eve dinner at a Chinese restaurant, they walked toward Times Square for the big countdown. The snow was gathering speed now, and the evening seemed a blur behind a shroud of dancing snowflakes, with neon signs changing in perpetual cycles and crowds of people pushing past each other like spools in and out of the weaving looms. Yet she felt secure and comfortable amid all that. *I am in the company of my beloved ones, and we stick together like an indivisible cluster. We are building our life together, not shivering in the snow. How lucky I am, delighted by what my life offers at this moment and every moment ahead of us. We each have so much to look forward to in the coming years.*

They returned to the hotel before midnight. There was no need to witness the celebration in Times Square; they were there, totally immersed in the spirit of a new beginning while letting go of the past. *I'll not allow myself to indulge in remorse and depression anymore, nor will I let self-doubt and fear of uncertainty dominate my life.*

The next morning, she drove her daughter to the airport. With sweet sorrow in her heart, she watched her big "little girl" walk into the terminal. Then she drove back to the client site. On her way, she passed by New Rochelle, and she reminisced about the fun time she had in La Rochelle, France, as a student so many decades before.

The Long Road to Recovery

What I'm going to tell you is a story with three different endings. It's about how a couple coped with the greatest devastation of their lives and what would have happened if they had chosen different paths.

∽

A young couple and their three kids lived in a suburb of a major city on the East Coast. The time was the late 1970s and early '80s.

The husband, in his late thirties, was a professional, working long hours in the office. Very often, his work spilled into the weekends.

The wife, in her early thirties, was a full-time mom. She kept the house tidy, and she shopped for the most nutritious food a single-income family could afford. Every day she took the kids for walks in their lower-middle-class neighborhood, and they went to the pool in the summer. She pinched every penny she could from the household expenses so that the family could take long vacations, such as camping trips in the mountains and overseas trips piggybacked on the husband's business trips.

Then calamity struck. Their nine-year-old boy, the eldest

child, was killed in an accident while riding his bike in the neighborhood. This horrible event was unimaginably devastating for the family. After that, the husband became completely taciturn, working even harder and isolating himself from others. The wife was gnarled by guilt and pain, mixed with anger and depression, which prevented her from performing her normal housekeeping and child-rearing functions.

One day, when the husband had come home late as usual, the wife had reached a state where she was bubbling with outrage and resentment, to the point that she couldn't help but release a torrent of sharp criticism at her husband. A rapid exchange of blame soon followed, primarily over the death of their child. That's what happened.

Scenario One

On impulse, the wife dashed out of the house, jumped into the car and drove away. Within a block of their house, she lost control of the car and hit a telephone pole. She was killed instantly. Running after the car, the husband was hit by a truck and taken to the hospital, where he died a week later. The two younger kids were taken into the custody of their grandparents, who lived thousands of miles away. They would never know their parents or learn what happened to them as the family kept silent about it.

Scenario Two

The couple sought professional help. Following the guidance of their counselor, the wife went back to school to get her professional training. Course after course, through tears and sweat, she completed her degree two years later and landed a job. Thanks to her extra income, the husband was more relaxed about his work. It was not easy to balance the family and two careers, but they recognized how lucky they were to have two children who gave them a reason to persist and carry on with their lives despite their pain and suffering.

Today, in their seventies, the couple has four grandchildren whom they see regularly. As they reflect on their life together, they see that it was a long journey from the most destructive event to a full recovery. They are grateful that they had the wisdom to choose the right path, and above all, the courage and patience to let time heal their wounds.

∽

What happened to this family was something between these two scenarios.

Soon after the accident, the family moved to a neighborhood far from the scene of their son's fatality. To all their new neighbors and friends, theirs was a typical family of a father, a mother, and two kids. All that reminded them of their dead child, including his pictures, was hidden away. While the children were quickly growing up under the summer sun, they were somehow overshadowed by a secret world in which the fading memories of their older brother hopped in and out.

One day the husband came home, depressed as usual. He suggested taking a trip back home, to where his parents lived. He wanted to pour his heart out to them, all the pain that he couldn't share with anyone, especially not his grief-stricken wife. The wife responded to his suggestion with hysteria, "If you want to visit your family, go by yourself then. I'm a total failure, I don't even have a job outside the home. I will not go back unless I am a worthy mother."

Eventually, following the advice and a great deal of nudging from her best friend, who was a psychiatric social worker, the wife went to a therapist and started a professional training program at the local community college.

While the husband was very supportive of his wife, watching the kids while she studied, he himself remained bottled up. He wanted his wife to succeed, yet he denied himself the chance to be free of the yoke of guilt and pain. Outside his immediate home, he was secretive and silent about the tragic episode, and he didn't allow anyone else to hint at it. One day, a colleague stopped by his office and expressed concerns over his mental well-being. A torrent of sobs suddenly burst from him, as if a floodgate had opened. Though he felt a lot better afterward, he couldn't share this incident with anyone, not even his wife. Life simply went on.

In a few years' time, the wife fulfilled her goal of achieving professional status. She landed a job with a prestigious firm, and year after year she moved up the ranks. She was so occupied with her demanding career that she could barely get around to managing her domestic life. As each day turned into a new day, each year into a new year, the sorrow and pain were sinking into the deep recesses of her soul.

On the surface, their life looked as normal as could be, and the kids grew up healthy and successful in school. With two incomes, the family was able to move to an elegant house in a desirable neighborhood. Yet the husband became more isolated from society. He hardly talked to any of his colleagues at work. No one understood what he felt. The passing of seasons only reminded him of the time of year when their first child was born, celebrations of birthdays and bar mitzvahs only caused him more sorrow as his child had barely made it to the age of nine. Gradually, he was excluded from the circle of office politics and was bypassed for his due promotion. He felt his struggles inside were not noticed or appreciated by his wife and children.

Entrapped in a suffocating downward spiral, he could only turn his anger and anxiety inward.

This situation finally reached a breaking point. While away on one of her overseas assignments, the wife received an unexpected call from a family friend: her husband had been hospitalized for internal bleeding. He had been diagnosed with cancer.

She took the first flight home and spent the entire journey in tears— tears of remorse for not paying enough attention to her family, tears of worry over what might happen, tears of anxiety about what she would do without the person who had walked by her side for so many years. From the airport, she went straight to the hospital.

Her husband opened his eyes, which were filled with tears, and managed to utter, "I'm so sorry."

"But why?"

"All these years, I should not have been bottled up about the loss of our child, and about the unfair situation at work."

After just three weeks, while waiting for a suitable bone marrow donor, he died, surrounded by his family. His last words to his children were, "Be magnanimous and be more tolerant with others."

> *My beloved died on an early spring night.*
> *His soul sailed through high mountains and shiny seas to the yonder land.*
> *It returns as a breeze gently touching my cheeks.*

∾

Overnight, the young woman was left to face her life alone, to shoulder the responsibilities of raising their growing children, paying two college bills and a large mortgage by herself.

Upon her husband's passing, she quit her overseas assignments so that she could be with her children, even though it took a great deal of effort to land a new job in the States. She couldn't accept that her husband's life had been cut short; she felt that she must find a way to keep his memory alive, so she established a scholarship fund in her husband's name. Through tears and sweat, and after many long hours of work, she made it, just as she had with her professional training decades earlier, after her child's passing.

Within a few years, the children graduated from college and moved on with their lives. She continued to thrive professionally.

Now retired and in her seventies, with both children married with their own families, she looks back: I'm grateful for everything I had, and for our remarkable children, even though one of them was only with us for nine years.

When she hears the cicadas humming incessantly and monotonously in the summer, she feels a pang in her heart, remembering their noise from the summer after her first child was born, and knowing that he would never hear it as the cicadas only return once every seventeen years. When she reads about the newly excavated tombs in China, her heart aches as she remembers the trip to the Silk Road that she and her husband took, and how they found the ancient Great Walls in the desert. How unbelievable that all those times are lost forever!

But at the same time she can see that their life together was just transformed into something different from what they'd expected. She also knows that, at the end of the rainbow in the night sky, he is always looking at her with tears in his eyes.

Sweetest Love, Do Not Go

You were an English person living in Holland; I was a Chinese person living in America. We met in remote Pakistan. By fate we met again and became soul mates for each other.

On that crisp autumn day, walking along the Thames, you asked me if I would always stay with you.

"Yes, I will," I said, without hesitation. "If I don't spend the rest of your life with you but someday find out you are no longer with us, I'd be more sorrowful."

With joy and trepidation in our hearts we began the most beautiful last chapter of our life. For more than ten years we became the very fabric of each other's existence. Reflecting on the happiness and sorrows in our past, we looked forward to a bright future together and grew more attached each day. As I drove to work, trees along the highway flew past the windows and clouds clung to the horizon, and all I could think of was what you were doing, what I wanted to tell you. Every time I returned from an out-of-town trip, whether it was clear or cloudy, snowy or windy, I could always spot you in the crowd waiting for me, your crown of silver hair, hands in your jacket pocket. There was never a shortage of things to talk about between us to simply express the joy in our hearts. In the warmth of your affection, tragic events of my life became things of the past; shadows of regrets, resentments, anger, sadness, and grief no longer lingered.

I often said, "How can I live without you?" You would reply, "I simply won't live without you!"

When we first met in Pakistan in 1992, I asked what interested you most as a consultant. You said, "To visit many places in the world and to understand different cultures more deeply." Coming from totally different cultures, we were irrevocably attracted to each other. Once I read an ancient Chinese poem, "Green, Green Grass on the Riverbank," which you found so charming that you set it to a song. Whenever a good book about China was published, you would read it before I did. If I showed interest in an English or American writer, you would brief me on his or her work and then find the books among those you had collected for my reading. No wander my sister said, "Look at you two, so connected with each other!" when she visited us in London.

When we met again five years after our initial acquaintance, you offered to write a piece of music for me. I suggested a song, but you ended up with forty-eight songs, each set to one of your favorite poems. Music was your lifelong aspiration. Only through music would you express your innermost feelings. Whenever a piece of good music played on the radio, you would grab the score from the bookshelf and follow it with the music. During the years of your retirement, you dedicated the most "sacred" morning hours to composing music. You wrote so much music that you certainly lived up to your aspiration, as you said, "I was born with eyes to read poems and ears to hear music; it's more important that I do what I want to do." When you worked on household chores, you would whistle simple, lovely tunes that instantly filled my heart with tender affection.

You were a great storyteller with an ingenuous sense of humor, and you had endless anecdotes to tell. These stories, while exotic and unbelievable, were far more interesting than anything I read.

There was the story of how you got lost in the safari while lions were roaring afar; there was the story of how you wandered among Bhutanese villages on high mountain ridges; there was the story of how you ascended to the Himalayan peak to see the sunrise.

We both loved nature. Together we shared some of the most beautiful sights on earth. We walked into the giant redwood forest as the sun seeped through the skyscraper treetops and cast a million rays like mosaics in a medieval cathedral; we observed the starry sky in an Australian vineyard, surrounded by total silence and darkness, trying to figure out the constellations from the southern hemisphere; we stepped onto Athabasca Glacier in the Canadian Rockies, awed by its thousand-foot depth and billion-year accumulation. Your cry of "it's worthy of my life just being here!" will always echo among the mountains and lakes.

We moved a number of times, from city to city, from country to country. Every time I asked you whether you felt isolated, you would say, "Why? Certainly not, as I am with my beloved wife." Every evening after the dinner table was cleaned, we would sit side-by-side watching episodes of BBC dramas. It was great fun chatting about the characters in the movies late into the night. For our daily meals, if I needed certain ingredients, you would get them right away. We didn't usually go to Chinese restaurants because you felt "my wife's cooking is far better than that."

While living in England, we bought a recipe book for making preserves. We would get the fruit from the market and work together, chopping, cooking, and bottling. The hard work was certainly worthwhile when we served our own marmalades and jams for breakfast. For Christmas, we would have the traditional English plum pudding. You would pour brandy on top of it and light a match to set it afire. When it was time for the major Chinese holidays we would get the year cake, moon cake, and rice wraps to commemorate the Chinese New Year, Moon, and Dragon Boat Festivals.

You were fondly referred to as "Lao Xian Sheng" ("Old Master") by my family. You were modest and respectful of others. All my friends who knew you thought highly of you for your gentle demeanor and even temperament. You enjoyed long-standing friendships from many parts of the world. For years, you never ceased sending financial support to the aging mother of your late wife. More importantly, you were so tolerant with me. You would advise me when I was critical to people, saying, "Don't be so hard on others." If I became argumentative, you would say, "I'll talk to you after you lower your voice by an octave."

I open the doors of the bookcases and see *Rembrandt's Eyes* given to you by my son, Ien, for your birthday. The miniature music pad from Shing, my daughter, is still lying on your desk, in which there are a few bars of your handwritten music. When we got married, both my children had just finished college. While you didn't have children of your own, you shared the burden of mine. "Your children love their mom very much." You would comfort me when I got upset with them. In Ien's first year at Cambridge, England, he brought a dozen friends over for an "all-American Thanksgiving." You took me to different shops to buy ingredients so we could put together a perfect Thanksgiving dinner. Yesterday, Shing called me from Philadelphia, and we reminisced about the time when we took her and her boyfriend, John, to Canterbury and other places. No doubt, you were an integral part of my children's growing up. You witnessed the completion of major milestones in their lives and were as proud of their achievements as any parent would be.

The understanding between us was beyond words spoken. Only you knew what I aspired to in life. Only you supported me wholeheartedly in achieving it. It was you who encouraged me to write the memoir of my parents. It was you who accompanied me to mainland China to gather information and to interview friends and family members. When my story was published in

Biographical Literature in Taiwan, it was you who was genuinely delighted in the fulfillment of my wish. Whenever I encountered difficulties at work, it was you who patiently listened to my complaints. I'd consult you for everything, even for what I should wear each morning. Whenever I took an out-of-town business trip, you would try your best to accompany me. Last October, I arrived in the UK from Germany during my two-week assignment. As soon as I was settled in the hotel room, I heard two soft knocks on the door. I opened the door and there you were. How very happy I was to see you!

∽

My dearest one, I cannot believe and I cannot accept that you are gone, in just an instant. In the darkness of night, I see you smile at me. When I return home from work exhausted, I slump into the couch. I feel your hands pull me up, I hear your voice saying, "Min-Hwa, Darling, it's time for dinner now; eat first, then go to sleep." I walk on the street; your outline against the green trees moves toward me in big strides. As a snowstorm rages outside, I hear you calling, "Come home, my dear! If you don't leave work now, you won't make it back." In the crowd, I instinctively extend my hand for you to lead me through the zebra line. When I weep, I hear you sigh. When I mourn, I see sadness in your eyes. When I sleep, you drift in from the window with the morning breeze and gently touch my cheeks. My love, you did not go! You will be with me as always, leading me, holding me, through the snowy ground in deep winter, the green pasture in early spring, the scorching sun in midsummer. You will walk with me on the falling leaves, over the slippery rocks in rushing streams, through the dark murky swamps until the end of the journey. How I look forward forever to that day, the day when I reach and open that door, when you will be there waiting for me.

Two Paintings

My father had two paintings by Fu Bao Shi (1904–1965), a prominent figure painter and landscapist of China's modern period. In 2012, ninety of his paintings were exhibited in the New York Metropolitan Museum of Art.

When I was a little girl living in Taiwan, I loved to sneak into my father's study. Along with a big desk with a green writing pad, a leather couch that opened into a bed, ink brushes pinned to a weight-bearing pole, and bookcases with sliding glass doors, were my father's paintings and calligraphies on the walls. I would stare at them for hours. The one I liked the most was a vertical scroll with three figures, one old man and two young women in ancient costume, each holding an instrument. They sat on the ground facing each other like a family of musicians. The girl facing outward was playing the flute while the other two listened to her. The old man's cheeks were slightly sunken and his eyes downcast; I could feel a certain melancholic mood coming out of the scroll. The strokes of the painting were simple and yet so powerfully expressive that the long sleeves seemed to move like a triple-looped numeral eight. This was one of the two Fu Bao Shi paintings in the house. The other was in the living room, on top of the open doorframe facing the back garden. It was a small "mountain and water" (Chinese for "landscape") painting. What interested my childish eyes was a young page carrying an oversized instrument, waddling along the mountain ridge while his master was enjoying the scenery with a friend. This idyllic picture of living in harmony with nature stirred up endless imagination and unnamed yearning in me.

For us, Fu Bao Shi was always "Uncle Fu." Father and Fu were close friends during the Sino-Japanese war (1937–1945) when the two families lived in Chongqing, the wartime capital in Southwest China. They were both from Jiangxi province and only one year apart in age, and above all, they shared a common interest in Chinese art. While my father was the dean of Zhengzhi University, Fu was a high school art teacher. Both families lived in remote villages in mountainous areas less exposed to the intense daily bombardments.

One day, my father visited Fu and stayed overnight. As usual, they talked throughout the night. Since my father was an accomplished calligrapher in his own right, and Fu specialized in the painting style that emphasizes brush strokes, Fu was most appreciative of my father's critique of his work. In parting, my father said to his friend, "My wife would come along if it weren't for her condition; she is too pregnant with our 'number three.' How regretful she must be not having the chance to admire your work!"

To my father's delight, Mr. Fu offered, "I don't have anything for you to bring home; just take a couple of paintings to your wife, any pieces to your liking."

After my father decided on two pieces among many scrolls, the artist inscribed a few lines on the paintings to commemorate the occasion, as was the tradition.

My parents never parted with these paintings.

Soon after the war with the Japanese ended, the civil war between the Communists and the Nationalist government raged. The paintings traveled with the family from Chongqing to

Nanjing, then to Shanghai, and finally to Taiwan. For decades, no one in Taiwan had any contact with the mainland. From time to time, my parents would talk about Fu Bao Shi as he was gaining fame in mainland China.

Year after year, the paintings stayed on the walls, while the world changed around them. The flutist stopped playing when my mother died in 1960 at the age of forty-four. The old man became ever more melancholic as my father lay sleepless on the leather sofa bed night after night. While the little page on the mountain path remained a young boy, the seven children of the master were leaving home, one by one, for foreign lands in search of their own paths. That idyllic setting of mountains touched with the gentle colors of autumn foliage was a world that could never be regained. Father died in 1982 during one of his trips visiting his children in the US. He was buried in Los Angeles. Later that year, we all went back to Taiwan for his memorial service.

Father left no will, much less a plan for the disposition of his collection of art and calligraphy. The house was now empty. Of the seven of us, only Zheng, the second son, traveled between Taiwan and China for business. He kept the house as a home base and leased it to a relative who was widowed with two school-age children. It seemed a good arrangement to have someone living in the house. We were all too busy to be concerned about the artwork in my father's study.

Father didn't own the house. It was allotted to our family when we moved to Taiwan several decades earlier. As time went by, the house looked increasingly diminutive amidst the sprouting high-rises. The small stall that sold breakfast at the corner of the street gave way to a proper restaurant. The sheds clinging to the walls of big houses were transformed into full-size stores. One day the inevitable happened; the government took over the house. And before long, a new building was in its place, obliterating the entire neighborhood beyond recognition. The paintings and its owner were forgotten.

When I visited Taiwan in 2004 for the publication of my parents' story I wrote for a magazine, I met Brother Zheng for lunch. He mentioned that Father's Fu Bao Shi paintings were on display in an exhibition commemorating the painter's one-hundredth birthday.

"Where are they now? Who has the paintings after all those years?" I asked Brother Zheng.

"When Mother was ill, Father sold them; he was hard-up for money."

"Do you know who bought them?"

"No idea."

I went to the Exhibition Hall without delay. Among a roomful of large and colorful scrolls, I spotted Father's paintings right away. The landscape painting was now at eye level; I could see all its details. For the first time I was able to read the inscription word by word, which described my father's visit to the artist's cottage in the fall of 1943. It felt strange to see the paintings in the exhibition. It was like opening our living room to the whole world. It also struck me that I was peeping into my parents' life before my own birth, sadly, so many years after their death. Like many paintings in the exhibition, a sign of "Private Collection" was displayed underneath them. I left the Exhibition Hall without finishing the exhibition, unable to describe what I felt: disbelief, anger, regret, guilt, or perhaps denial.

During the same trip, I had a long conversation with Gan, another brother of mine who was also traveling between China and Taiwan at the time. I asked if he saw Father's paintings in the Exhibition Hall.

"I certainly did," he replied with an attitude in his tone. "Do you know how these paintings got into the hands of others?"

"Brother Zheng said Father sold them because he needed money for mother's illness." I repeated what I had heard.

"I wouldn't believe a word of that." Gan turned forceful and indignant. "Mother died more than twenty years before Father. When we went back home for Father's memorial service in 1982, the paintings were still on the wall in Father's study."

But it was not as simple as that. Gan was my father's favorite and also his biggest headache. He returned to Taiwan after receiving a PhD in the US in the late 1970s. But with one trouble after another, mostly involving women and money, he brought my father nothing but embarrassment. On the contrary, Zheng was the son who took care of Father and the household matters all these years when the other siblings were away. Yet he didn't have the kind of academic achievements my father expected of his children. For one reason or another, the two brothers did not get along and were not on speaking terms for years.

Even as I tried very hard to recollect what I saw in the house during our 1982 trip, I couldn't say I noticed anything missing. The whole trip was a blur as I was completely inundated by jet lag, endless visits from friends and relatives, and too much food from too many parties. I didn't respond to Gan's accusation. After all, there were other people living in the house all these years. As I wrote about this, it occurred to me that my older sister, Da, had visited Father in Taiwan a couple of years before his death. She brought back with her many of Father's paintings and calligraphies, but Fu's paintings were not among them. Did that mean they were already gone during Father's final years?

When I returned to the US, I sent an email to Zheng: "Could you please buy me a catalog of Fu's Centennial Exhibition? I would like to have the photos of the two paintings that were part of our home and childhood."

Total silence ensued.

Years later, when I mentioned this incident to Long, the oldest of my seven siblings, he simply shook his finger as if to say, "I don't want to talk about it."

I was thus left wondering who the private collector of these paintings was and how he had obtained them. It was a mystery both frustrating and challenging! Yet I pushed it to the back of my mind like a box in the attic waiting for the right moment "when I have a chance to deal with it."

The box remained untouched for several years until one day I received an email from an acquaintance, with a link to a network of digital images of Fu's entire work. It was an art auction website operating in China, but the artwork could be anywhere in the world.

I didn't open the email right away. I didn't know why. Do I want to see these paintings again? What do I really want to find out? Did Father sell them for Mother's illness or for some other reason? Did someone take the paintings from the house? Who was that "private collector?" More importantly, would I be able to deal with the issue with my limited resources? Should I spend the rest of my life fighting for them? If we did recover the paintings, who among us would be entitled to them?

My parents had seven children in nine-and-a-half years. Jealousy and competition for parental affection never ended; bitter fights constantly erupted in our childhood. As we grew up, confrontations among the siblings hurt more deeply and left a bad taste for a long time. As the middle of seven children, I tried to stay uninvolved, assuming someone would take care of family affairs. Even if I wanted to help, I wouldn't be needed.

Could I blame any of my siblings for not taking care of the family legacy? Could I blame my father for not protecting his prized legacy? Did I do anything to prevent that from happening? Should I blame myself for not paying attention to Father in his final years?

No one would have the answers. My elder sister, Da, has been gone for many years and there are only six of us. The youngest has almost reached retirement age. Now it was time to open the box.

I went online and quickly located Father's paintings among seven volumes of Fu's artwork. There they were, in splendid form, magnificently displayed in front of me. The three musicians sit at a perfect angle to each other; the two friends on the cliff are admiring the autumn foliage through a thin veil of mountain mist. My father's name appears prominently in the painter's inscriptions on both paintings, which describe the memorable evening in a cottage on Golden Buddha Mountain as war was raging all over China.

Here, I met my father again, his youthful aspirations, his passion for beauty, and his many talents. He might have been moody and temperamental, he might have been intolerant and demanding, he might have made mistakes, but his love for his family never wavered. We were his pride and joy, no matter where we were or what we did. We inherited from him many of his attributes and qualities, as well as his shortcomings. These paintings are always my father's, and we are always my father's children, his most prized legacy.

Dajie and Me

I dreamt of Dajie two nights in a row, on March 9 and 10, a week before her passing. Since we parted as unmarried girls forty-two years ago, she has come to my dreams often, more than any other family member. This bond came from our childhood, the childhood beyond what's frozen in the family picture of a father, a mother, and seven children.

Dajie means "Big Sister." I am Xiaomei, the Little Sister. We were three years apart—three years less one month, to be exact. My big sister loved to remind everybody that we were only two years apart during this one month of the year. We were number two and number four of a family of four boys and three girls. Our shared childhood, as far as I can trace in my memory, took place mostly in Taiwan.

Dajie was affectionately called "Frog" by her friends because her formal name, Qing-Hua, sounds like "frog" in Chinese (Qing Wa). I was referred to as "Little Frog" by her friends, as I tagged along with this popular sister of mine. I was also the little sister she liked to boast about: "At the age of ten, Min-Hwa went to Second Girls' School, one of the magnet schools in Taipei. She even skipped the entrance exam and went straight from junior high to senior high."

I was not, however, without misgivings, growing up in my

sister's shadow. Once a friend of hers commented on my New Year's outfit: "How smart Little Frog looks in that pair of green trousers!"

Dajie quickly responded, "These used to be mine, but since I grew out of them, they were passed on to my sister."

I don't know why, but I was too sheepish to let her know that what she did was not fair. I turned the anger inward instead. Can't I even have a pair of new trousers for the New Year? I was upset with my parents for being so frugal; I was upset with them for making me the second girl, not the oldest or the youngest. Of course, I was most upset that my sister, as glamorous as she was, wouldn't even allow me a tiny taste of glory.

Dajie had her weak spot too, which she could be equally sensitive about. In our family, as in most Chinese families, children's education was paramount. In a system where students had to pass exams to progress from one level to the next, our only duty and obligation was to move up the education ladder. Passing exams at school was always a struggle for Dajie, although she demonstrated superb abilities in every other way. She was the first to ride a bicycle and the first to drive an automobile, just to name a few of her feats, and she had a clever and quick mind and fantastic powers of imagination.

Once, Dajie tried to teach me how to ride a bike, but I ended up in a ditch with shallow water. After that, I became a frequent fixture on the back rack of my sister's bicycle. Her strength grew as I grew taller and heavier. When I was fifteen, I became taller than Big Sister, something she was not very pleased about, not for the increased load on her bike but for the symbolic shift of our relative positions, although we remained Dajie and Xiaomei for the rest of our time together.

It was 1960, the final year of our mother's illness. Dajie was taking a gap year after high school, staying home to prepare for the college entrance exam. One day we made plans to hang out after I was finished with classes at school. When I walked to the school's front gate to meet my sister, I found her leaning against her bike in anguish.

"What's wrong?" I asked.

Tears came down as she told me that a middle-aged woman had come by and said to a group of students, "Look! This is a typical 'Tai Mei.'" "Tai Mei" means "the Bad Girl" in the most negative sense of the term. It must have been Big Mama Luo, the hateful director of student affairs, I thought. Fury hit me like a lightning bolt.

"Wait here. I'll take care of this." I dashed back to the school building, straight to the office of student affairs, and found Big Mama Luo chatting with people around her.

"Mrs. Luo, do you know who the girl outside the gate is?" My voice sounded as if it came from someone outside me. "She is my sister."

"Of course, I do, Ho Min-Hwa! You two look alike," she said, with a sinister smile, like a tiger's.

"Why did you call my sister 'Tai Mei?'" I was now amid the storm; I just had to go through with it.

"Why not? Just look at the way she is dressed."

Dajie was wearing a sweater and a pair of light-blue jeans. Her hair was long and braided, a clear sign that she was out of school (at that time in Taiwan it was mandatory that all schoolgirls keep their hair short and straight). Above all, my sister had a figure that was unarguably shapelier than that of most schoolgirls in uniform.

"Let me tell you, Mrs. Luo," I exclaimed, before the room full of people, "you should be respectful to my sister, and to anybody for that matter." I walked quickly out of the office, leaving behind me a Big Mama Luo in shock.

Dajie and I decided to go home instead of hanging out—we

were no longer in the mood for it. We walked slowly side by side, dragging the bike along by its handlebars. In reflecting upon what had happed, I grew worried. I knew full well that I could be dismissed by the school for misconduct. What if that happens? Well, I could always go to another school. Wait a minute, who would take someone with a bad record? I'm only one-and-a-half years from graduation. If I don't have a high school diploma, I won't be able to take the once-a-year college entrance exam. What should I do? Father would kill me if he knew. Yet, I don't regret what I did. I had to defend Dajie, who is staying home for the year because she failed her college entrance exam last summer, and I cannot imagine how this incident will affect her self-confidence. We talked and talked; the issue was still hanging over us.

When we arrived home, Father was with Mother by her sickbed. Mother noticed something was wrong. Tearfully, I said to them both, "We were bullied at school." This opening quickly brought them to our camp. I told them the whole story. Father was uncharacteristically calm, no scolding or lecturing as we had expected. He only asked the name of the director in question. Then he put on his shoes and wool hat, took his ubiquitous English gentleman's walking cane, and left the house.

An hour or so later, he returned, equally calm but with a hint of giddiness in his expression. "I met with that director of yours. All is resolved." My heart sang. My father is marvelous, I knew it, I always knew it.

"I met with Mrs. Luo and we had a brief talk. I found out she was from a certain university in Sichuan during the war. I told her I had taught and served as the dean of students at Zheng-Zhi University and knew most of the faculty at her university."

"What happened then?" I couldn't wait for the answer.

"She turned red all over." That's the end of the story.

The summer after that incident, Dajie made her second attempt at the college entrance exam and got into Danjiang

College, one of the private colleges. A year later, I graduated from Second Girls' School and went on to National Taiwan University, the most prestigious college in Taiwan.

Around that time, Mother passed away after a prolonged bout with ovarian cancer. Father, full of grief, faced the daunting task of raising seven children, aged from ten to nineteen, alone. He couldn't trust anyone to run the household. Eventually, Dajie was asked to take on that responsibility. She was only eighteen, having just started her much-anticipated college life.

What Father needed was not a housekeeper, but a person of accountability. Dajie presided over a team of a servant/cook and seasonal helpers. During the brief period when Father was appointed the vice chairman of the then-nascent Taiwan SEC, we had a car with a driver, which Dajie had the full power to dispatch. Father relied on her as a bridge between himself and us, as he was more comfortable with her.

Dajie took her role seriously, but she was nonetheless resentful about it. She thought she had been saddled with a domestic role because of her underperformance at school. "Why doesn't Xiaomei do some work too?" was a constant nag.

The few years after Mother's death, from 1960 until 1966, when Dajie and I left home for Belgium, was a difficult period for us all, having lost our mother while growing from adolescence into adulthood. Dajie became the Little Mother for her younger brothers and sisters. Every evening the kids got together at the dining table, cramming for exams. She would scramble together enough money to buy a pot of noodles at Mr. Chou's noodle shop. To our growing bunch it tasted as good as anything that gold could buy. Dajie could also be a rival to her siblings at the same time. When fights erupted between siblings, she was either with "us" or "them."

Dajie was proud of her little brothers and sisters when it came to our studies. She was relentless in making us do our best. A year after Mother's death, I took my college entrance exam in the sweltering heat of a Taiwan summer. Every day during the examination week, my sister brought me a freshly cooked lunch, including soup in a thermos flask, while other students waited for their parents. It was a morale booster in a race with tens of thousands of competitors. In the end, I not only passed the exam, I also earned the second highest scores of that year.

During one of my college years, I had a summer job translating documents from English to Chinese for a publishing company, which paid for the pieces translated. When the summer was over, I planned to return unfinished work without pay, but Dajie insisted that I finish it. "You should not have accepted them if you couldn't finish them," she said. I recounted this story to my sister during my last visit with her, and I told her I was grateful for her interference.

Above all the characteristics that she possessed, Dajie was a fighter, and a mighty one; she had to win, and she would win at any cost. Her goal was not to benefit herself but to defeat her opponent. Once, her best friend asked both of us to meet a "special friend," on whom she had a serious crush. He was indeed an impressive prospect, a charmer with broad shoulders. At the end of that encounter, it became clear that the "Prince on the White Horse" was head over heels for my sister, who was not only beautiful but also masterful in applying her charms. What a spectacular row the two friends had afterward! Dajie didn't budge, saying, "I, too, like him." But she didn't keep her trophy for very long; she lost interest in him as soon as the battle was won.

Dajie was fiercely competitive in the areas that matter most to young girls. When we were studying in Belgium, one of the few French sentences she could master was, "Qui est la plus vieille?" ("Guess who is the older one?") She was pleased that nine times out of ten, people would guess I was the older one, as I was two full inches taller. It didn't matter to her how much her delight affected her younger sister's self-image. That was the way she was: born to win.

During that era, if a college graduate in Taiwan wanted to go abroad for graduate or professional studies, he or she had to pass a difficult exam. Dajie found a way around it. She somehow made the acquaintance of two Belgian nuns who were looking for girls to go to Belgium, with the aim of bringing them to missionary work. Eager to leave Taiwan and our "uninspiring" lives behind, we both signed up. It turned out that our destination was a boarding school run by the convent of Les Soeurs de la Croix, not a proper university with graduate studies. For Dajie, it was an expedient way of going abroad. For me, it was a deviation from the path of serious studies. For many years afterward, I considered going to Belgium with Dajie a significant mistake in my life.

In Belgium, while we had two totally different objectives, we were stuck with each other. Deficient in French, Dajie turned that disadvantage into a winning tactic: she was able to maximize her other abilities beyond the language boundary. I was the interpreter when needed; she was the director behind the scenes. I felt helplessly victimized, constantly subject to her plots and schemes. We parted after two semesters. I went to Paris to pursue a French language degree at the Sorbonne, and she went to the States to marry SL, whom she had met in Taiwan.

In the ensuing four decades, we each moved on and created our own worlds. Dajie was a warm and generous hostess when I visited. She was caring toward my children and genuinely supportive when I was down. Yet Dajie never changed. She had to command and control; she had to win and defeat others; she had to be the center of attention and affection. My new roles in life, as a wife, mother, and professional, transformed me from a little sister who could only turn her anger and resentment inward into an adult who could think independently and assert her own will. Yet I couldn't help being apprehensive every time Dajie tried to exercise her power to influence and dominate some aspects of my life. Even though she was in her world, far from mine, those encounters could be as hurtful and upsetting as ever.

The summer after my husband's death, I made a trip with my children from our home in Maryland to visit my uncle in Geneva, who was the Chinese commissioner to the UN and with whom I had had close contact for many years. Once she learned of the plan, Dajie immediately organized a trip with her daughter, a Wall Street financial analyst, to join us. For the few days of our visit in Geneva, she did all she could to get attention from the person whom she had despised as a "traitor" (our uncle had returned to China after the Communist takeover in 1949). She succeeded in diverting the affection and comfort from my uncle that my children and I sought in our bereavement. Dajie just couldn't tolerate that anyone else, especially not her little sister, might be the center of attention.

Last spring, when the news came that cancer had spread to her brain and brain surgery was imminent, I said to myself, "Dajie has fought ovarian cancer for the past ten years; she survived it and will make it again this time." She was invincible to all who knew her, not just her little sister. Yet my daughter, a physician, urged me, "Ma, go see Big Auntie. She will not be around forever. If you have any scores to settle with her, do it now." I took an overnight trip from the East Coast to Los Angeles. We talked about our childhood memories and my feelings of ambivalence about our long-standing resentment toward each other. She listened and was uncharacteristically quiet.

She survived that surgery for another half a year. In February 2009, doctors stopped all treatments. On my way back to Los Angeles, I said to myself, "She is dying," but I dreaded facing it. When I saw her, I knew I had done the right thing by coming. She wanted to see me and was happy I was there for her.

The surgery and subsequent radiation therapy had significantly impaired her speech and mobility. She could only speak in short sentences, but they were full sentences that expressed her intent and emotions well. She was carried in a wheelchair to and from the bed and the toilet, from the bedroom to the kitchen, and from the living room to the car.

The morning after my arrival, I helped her with a morning snack, a box of roasted chicken wings brought in by her walking club buddies. I broke the chicken into small pieces and put them into her mouth, one by one. "I can eat the whole box," she managed to say. She wanted me to know how much she enjoyed being nursed by me. This sudden realization filled my heart with tenderness. If I had only known that the tender care from her siblings was what she had craved, even though she had always played the nurturing role.

A couple of her friends came to the house while she was resting. She tried to talk. "This is my sister, Min-Hwa. She writes well …" She stopped and looked frustrated, as she couldn't finish what she wanted to say. She wanted to tell her friends about the story I had written and published a few years before. I knew it. She was our sister, the Little Mother who had been so proud of us when we were young.

In the afternoon, she and I went outside, with a nurse pushing her wheelchair. We walked around the posh neighborhood of Palos Verdes Estates. With the Pacific Ocean on the horizon far beyond, I marveled at the world she had painstakingly built against all odds over the past four decades. Her husband had been in and out of jobs, and she was the one who created a home business to keep a Californian upper-middle-class lifestyle.

She wasn't enjoying the fresh air and scenery. She was sad and depressed; sad because she was to leave this world she loved, and depressed because she couldn't win the fight against the illness. I asked her, "Are you tired, Dajie?" She nodded. "Do you want to go home?" She nodded again.

On Sunday, her husband dressed my sister in a casual shirt and a pair of trousers in preparation for a Chinese New Year celebration hosted by their friends. I rummaged around and found a designer hat that matched her outfit. When I put it on her, she smiled.

Our arrival at the restaurant with my sister in a wheelchair brought sudden silence to a room full of chatter. Dajie maintained her composure by saying, "Happy New Year" to those she knew. Some responded with a few words; many seemed to consider my sister a ghost and simply avoided us. My sister had always been at center stage; how infuriated she must have felt to be neglected, and by her friends. Yet we stayed until the end of the party. She didn't ask to leave. She wanted to show the others that she was not a quitter.

When we returned home, her house seemed sober and dim compared with the sunny day outside, and it was uncomfortably still without Dajie's boisterous babbling and laughter and usual loud commands. I opened the fridge full of food, leftovers mixed with everything else. I wanted to tell my sister how much I longed for the special dishes she used to prepare. In the garden, oranges hung seductively on the tree branches and tropical plants stood around the swimming pool. I recalled how Jan, my second husband, and I had helped Candace (Dajie's younger daughter) bury her pet dove in the garden, shortly after our honeymoon in Las Vegas. I wanted to talk about Jan and show her the photo in which he and I stood under the cherry blossoms, so much in love with each other. I wanted to tell her how much the pain weighed on my heart and how lonely I felt after his passing. I wanted to pour all my tears over her shoulders for the sorrows in my life. Then I thought, "But she cannot say much, and she cannot do anything now; and she won't be around much longer."

Before she was to retire, I ordered the airport shuttle for

the following morning. " I will leave for the airport first thing tomorrow, Dajie."

"I know," she nodded.

"It's so hard for me to say goodbye."

"It's harder for me, very hard."

It was all told without words. She was the sister who taught me how to ride a two-wheel bike. She was the sister who took me on the back rack of her bike and pedaled fiercely forward. She was the sister whom her little sister latched onto while nervously watching the ground shifting faster and faster beneath the pedals.

My maternal grandfather Dr. Qiu Ji Shen, my maternal uncle, Dr. Qiu Shi Xin, and my mother Qiu Shi Fu

My mother and her brother in Hangzhou, circa 1935-37

My mother as a teenager, circa 1930

My mother as an unmarried
young woman, circa 1935

My mother in Beijing opera costume, circa 1930-1935

My father Professor He Chee Shin, circa 1930-1935

My father, circa 1935-1940

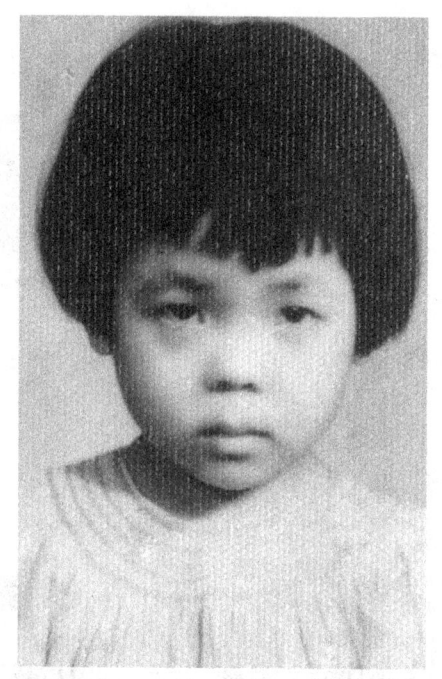

My first photo, circa 1946-1947

Our family in Taiwan, circa 1952

My first husband Dr. Chung-chieh Cheng and I cruising Three Gorges on the Yangzi in 1993

My husband and I in Dun Huang China, 1994

My second husband V Jan Kennard OBE and I in New Haven, CT 2002 before my daughter's wedding.

V J Kennard in Grand Teton, WY 2002

My husband Chung-chieh at home in Potomac, MD

My son Guang-Yeu at the age of nine.

Seven Lunch Boxes

My granddaughter, Maxine, fascinates me to no end. Every time I visit my daughter and her family in Philadelphia, I must make a mental adjustment, even after a short interval of a few weeks. At the age of eighteen months, she can sing, she can run, she can climb up and down. I take her to school in the morning. She leads me to the kitchen corner and, with fine gestures and baby talk, she makes me put her lunch and snacks in the fridge. Her teacher greets us with a big smile, saying, "Maxine has the best lunch in the class. Her mom always prepares her fancy lunches and snacks with so many varieties."

The wheel of time rolls back a half century before when I was a child growing up in Taiwan. Six days a week, we kids went to school at the crack of dawn and did not return home until dusk. Classes started immediately after a thirty-minute physical drill and continued with brief recesses in between. As always, hunger crept in before noon, and food was the only thing churning in my head. As soon as the lunch bell rang, two classmates went to the school kitchen where our lunch boxes were re-heated over a huge pot of boiling water. When the lunch boxes were brought back to the classroom, jostling against some fifty classmates, I found mine, a five-by-seven-by-two aluminum box. I untied the cord around it and lifted the lid despite the finger-burning heat. What a lovely sight! Against a background of steamed rice, there were edamame peas with mustard greens, shiny like a pile of jade; a pocket egg stuffed with meat and other treasures; a piece of vegetarian chicken made with layers of tofu sheets; the red braised pork begging to be tasted; and wow ... the fried eel! Mother's signature dish! How crispy it was, even after re-heating!

My mother was most keen to feed us with a balanced diet. Even with a couple of domestic helpers at her disposal, she always prepared our meals herself. Every morning, as the first ray of dawn passed through the windowpanes, I'd wake up to the aroma of food and the sound of Mother's busy steps in the kitchen. As soon as we got dressed for school, the breakfast would be waiting on the round table in the dining room, with steamed cake, soy milk, rice porridge, pickled vegetables, and salty eggs.

I loved the steamed cake, hot to the touch, spongy at every bite, and irresistible in taste. Each day, Mother saved a small amount of dough as a starter for the next day. If the starter went bad she would lament, "What a headache!". We didn't like milk because the only kind available then was powdered milk. Mother made her own soy milk to supplement the calcium need of her growing children. She had a miniature stone mill installed in the kitchen. It was about one foot in diameter, made of two stone disks, one on top of the other, connected by an axis in the middle. The disk at the bottom was a few inches larger and its extra space was carved into a U-shaped trench. The soybeans, which had been soaked overnight, were poured into the hole on the top. Mother's helper would rotate the stones in one direction with the handle attached to the axis, and the flow of milk-like liquid would come through between the two disks and then into the receptacle. The soy milk would be boiled and slightly sweetened to make a drinkable beverage. To this day, I swear that nothing tastes better than the soy milk fresh from our home soy mill.

The lunch boxes would always be ready when we finished breakfast. We would each grab a box and squeeze it into our overloaded book bag while running out the door for school. At first, only four of us—my two older brothers, my older sister, and I—needed lunch boxes for school. The number of boxes increased each year as younger kids turned school age. Mother would get up earlier and earlier to prepare our lunch boxes.

In the fifties, gas stoves were not widely used in Taiwan. In our household, the "coal ball" was the primary source of fuel for cooking. It was made of coal chips pressed into a cylinder about six inches in diameter and eight inches in height. Inside each cylinder, many finger-sized holes allowed air to flow through. Two coal cylinders, stacked on top of each other in a stove designed exclusively for burning coal balls, made up what amounts to a modern-day oven with a stove top. The fire was ignited from the bottom cylinder and went through the holes to reach the top one. Before one of them was burned out, it would be crucial to replace it with a fresh one. If bad luck struck, both coal cylinders could burn out; the family would then be out of fire for cooking. As far as I can recall, until Mother fell ill, we never missed our lunch boxes.

Despite her training in Chinese medicine under the tutelage of her own father, Dr. Qiu Ji Shen, the renowned medicine man in Zhejiang province, she never worked outside the home. She was also an accomplished Chinese opera singer in her youth who had given charity performances during the eight-year Sino-Japanese War. In that era, artists from good family background were not supposed to work for a living. My father used to tell us, "Your mother had never set foot in the kitchen before she married me; now she can put together a banquet in a moment's notice." Yet, every time Father commented the professional accomplishments of some women of his acquaintance, Mother would be deeply pained, as she thought she would never live up to her husband's standard of a Superwoman.

I don't remember how we got along with our day-to-day life after Mother was diagnosed with ovarian cancer. I had barely turned thirteen. There were no more holiday feasts at home and our lunches were simply consolidations of leftovers from dishes prepared by helpers. Eventually, I obtained permission to eat at the school kitchen with the staff who didn't have families. The food was abominable, but I survived, only sadly. We all survived, my brothers, my sisters, and I.

After dinner, bath, and bedtime routines, Maxine is now in bed. My daughter is still busy preparing the lunch and snacks for her little girl.

"You had a hectic day in the hospital," I said, "why don't you take it easy for a while?"

"Ma, when we were little, didn't you always make our baby food from scratch? How can I feed my daughter with ready-made baby food?"

My mother died at the age of forty-four. She didn't live long enough to see any of her seven children grow up. She would be very pleased to know that her grandchildren and great-grandchildren, who never had the chance to meet her, have continued her legacy.

Grandmother's Food Wagon

Not having heard from her daughter for a couple of days, she picked up the phone and touched the FaceTime icon. "It's after eight in the evening," she thought, "she should be home by now."

To her surprise, it was the girls who appeared on the screen.

"Grand mommy!" The twelve-year-old showed up first, then the nine-year-old, with a big grin showing two gaps among her front teeth.

"I dialed your mom's number, how come you girls answered the phone?"

"Mom's not at home. We can answer calls on our iPad."

"Where is your mom?"

"She's at work."

Since the onset of coronavirus in Washington, everyone has been on edge, waiting for the onslaught of this deadly disease. The girls' school closed on the first week of March; the students have been taking classes at home. Businesses in the city were closing one by one.

"Still at work?"

"Yeah."

"Hmm. Is she seeing patients?"

"I guess so." The twelve-year-old raised her eyebrows as if to say, That's the way it goes. "Last night, she didn't get back until eight and went to bed right away, exhausted."

It sounded serious.

Her daughter is a physician at the Fred Hutchinson Cancer Research Center. As a pulmonologist, she sees patients during clinic hours in addition to her all-consuming research projects. In this unprecedented situation, she had to pitch in as needed as well as provide treatment guidelines. "It was real now! My daughter was fighting on the frontlines of the war against the pandemic."

She felt her heart wrench.

Seattle has gone through a roller-coaster ride. With a less spectacular surge of deaths in recent weeks, one would speculate that it had passed the peak, at least in this area. Yet it still bothered me to think about how ill-equipped the hospitals were and how many healthcare workers were infected.

She took a deep breath, trying to reassure myself: it's all right, just hope for the best. She will be careful. After all, my daughter has been trained to save lives, why wouldn't she protect herself from harm?

The phone call from my daughter twenty-four years before was still ringing in her ears. "Ma, I got into UCSF medical school! I think I'll accept the admission."

"Don't you want to wait until you hear from other schools?"

"Ma, don't you know UCSF is among the top medical schools in the nation? I'm tired of the cold weather on the East Coast. Four years in Boston is enough. Can't wait for a change. Do you think Daddy would have approved of it?" Her father had passed away a year earlier when she was a sophomore at Harvard, something that was still very hard for her to accept.

So, she went to medical school in San Francisco, then to an internship, a residency, and a fellowship at Yale and University of Pennsylvania. She worked as an attending physician in Philadelphia and a research physician in Seattle, with a normal share of highlights and setbacks on the way, including a one-year break from medical school, marriage to someone who was also pursuing a medical career, and raising two daughters.

The bond between the mother and daughter deepened as she grew from one stage to another. On one Mother's Day, the daughter sent her mother a card printed with "The Child's Bath" by Mary Cassatt. "Happy Mother's Day, dear Mommy. I picked this card because I imagine this is how tender you were with me when I was a little girl."

When the mother remarried and moved to London, the daughter experienced a fit of anxiety. Not expecting such a violent reaction, the mother realized that her daughter would always be her baby, no matter how grown up she became. She made the effort to fly back and forth between London and San Francisco, despite her demanding job with a UK company, to assure her child that her mother would always be there when needed.

In her daughter's final year of med school, she sent her a card, saying, "Dear Mommy, this year I send you a card with two women arm in arm, because now that I'm not a baby anymore, I know that I can confide in you since we have the special friendship of mothers and daughters …"

Since then, many Mother's Days have come and gone. Her little girl has become a mother herself, the center of her own universe, and now she is the grandmother of two little girls.

Yet her daughter has always been her little girl, even though she is strong enough to deal with human suffering daily. She was struck with mixed emotions when she saw her daughter bulging with a five-month pregnancy for the first time. How could my child be shouldering all the burdens of motherhood?

For her, grand motherhood was a steep learning curve, to carry the warm soft bundle in a Baby Björn, to push the stroller through the cobblestoned streets, and to play hide-and-seek with two toddlers among the shrubberies. And it amazed her as much as it delighted her when the squirmy soft bundle could now carry her grandmother on her back and help her make scallion pancakes.

Her daughter called as soon as she heard that the governor of Washington announced the stay-at-home order. "Stay where you are, Ma! Don't go out. The situation will get worse before it gets better."

"What about the girls? Don't you want me to take care of them while you are both working in the hospital?" Her husband, a surgeon at the University of Washington, also had both clinical and research duties.

She felt torn. With both mom and dad out, the girls would end up eating junk food. She knew her daughter, a good cook, would like to feed her children meals made from scratch, but not when she was exhausted after a twelve-hour day at the ICU.

"Ma, don't worry about us. John and I will cover for each other."

The roles had changed. The daughter felt she must carry her mother in a crisis, ensuring her safety. But as her child's mother, she also wanted to walk with her daughter arm in arm during this difficult time.

Looking at the two darling faces on her phone, she quickly recovered from her reveries. "What would you like to eat that only Grand mommy can make?"

"Let's think about it."

An email came the next day: "Dear Grand mommy, we would like to have the egg and meat rolls. We haven't had it for a while." It's ground meat wrapped in a sheet of egg pancake. What a great idea! She replied immediately.

Ding! Ding! Ding! The doorbell rang. It was the Grand mommy food wagon. A bag of food was left by the front door with a note: "What is the next order?"

Tiny Tears

Ten days ago, Grandmother, Mother, and two girls left Seattle for Taipei, Taiwan. The plan was for the girls, aged eleven and eight, to attend a four-week Chinese language camp there. The family rented an apartment near the school. The grandmother was to stay for the first part of the four weeks, and the father would join the family later. Now, the grandmother was leaving. Bags had been packed, followed by a simple dinner of assorted leftovers, topped off with a fresh bunch of plump, succulent lychees. There was still more than two hours to go before the airport limo would show up.

Grandmother opened a roll of writing paper she had bought earlier that day, the kind specifically designed for Chinese calligraphy, printed with rows, columns, and diagonal lines. She soaked the writing brush in a cup of cold water and took out the ink stone from its ornate case. Her two young helpers surrounded her, busily making the ink. They rubbed the ink stone with an ink stick and a bit of water while bombarding their grandmother with all sorts of questions: What is the ink stick made of? Why does it make the ink black?

Grandmother dipped the brush into the ink and painted six characters on the far left column of the paper: 一, 二, 三, 四, 五, 六 (1, 2, 3, 4, 5, 6). The girls followed her brush with their eyes, eagerly waiting their turn to write their "columns." Once the paper was filled up and the ink dry, it was put on the wall, ready to receive its due homage.

Suddenly, the phone rang. The entire family had the same reaction: "It's only 7:15 p.m., too early for the limo." But the call was from the driver. "Given that a strike is going on in the airport," Grandmother said, "it's better to be safe than sorry. I might as well leave now." She quickly put on her jacket.

Not ready for the unexpected departure, the younger sister burst into tears, clutched at Grandmother, and buried herself in her bosom. The older sister tried to comfort her sister as tears welled up in her eyes.

"Goodbye, my angels, I will miss you every minute of my waking hours," said Grandmother as she hurried down three flights of stairs to meet the waiting driver.

Flying over the Pacific, surrounded by the soft sound of breathing in the darkness of the Boeing 777 cabin, she felt strange without the usual giggling and laughter around her. She opened the window shade and saw the stars solemnly positioned against the fathomless dark sky. The image of her little girls' tears turned her eyes misty, making the stars twinkle. "How I miss them!" she sighed.

> I miss our daily walks to and from school. We walked on tree-lined boulevards, and we walked through narrow winding alleys. We walked under the scorching sun, and we walked in torrential rain. We walked to my old neighborhood, altered beyond recognition today, to find the site of the house where I spent my growing-up years. We stopped at the fruit shop, dazzled by the glorious display of mangos, melons, papayas, and many unnamed exotic fruits.

I miss having my daily meals with my family, whether it was the scallion pancakes from the street vendor, the beef noodles, salmon fried rice, or a nine-course banquet in a fancy restaurant. What a pleasure it was seeing two hungry little hippos gobble up a half-dozen stuffed buns for breakfast and being part of their hilarious mirth over an enormous pile of mango smoothie!

I miss our evenings at home, watching silly animated movies or working on homework. I was the proudest grandmother when they asked me to sign at the bottom of their homework assignments.

I miss our weekend outings. We visited the rare collections of Chinese arts in the National Palace Museum, marveling at the sixth-century paintings together. We were equally awed by the room-size waterlilies painted with huge ink strokes. In Yangmingshan Park, where my parents used to take my brothers, sisters, and me for day trips, we traced the old steps to the spot where we could see the Danshui River snaking around the city. It was wonderful to watch two energetic kids running around on the moss-covered paths and chasing after the butterflies, just as I had done many decades before!

The airplane was now crossing the international date line. It flew from the dark side of the hemisphere into the light. The morning kept progressing as the plane moved eastward. Someone lifted a window shade, and a flood of golden rays rushed in. "It is now the morning of yesterday!" she exclaimed. "We are back to the past."

Indeed, this trip reconnected me to the past, wherever I was, in the air, in the sound, in the smell, and in the taste. This is the world I used to come home to, and this is the world I had lost for so long.

> I see a little girl wandering about in the meandering alleys between the school and her home. I see this girl spend her last pennies buying a pencil with a doll's head to make a standing Barbie. I see a growing girl eager to open her lunch box prepared by her loving mother every morning. I see a teenage girl cramming for college entrance exams in the sweltering heat of summer. I see a young college student climbing to the mountaintop to pick the tips of tea leaves. I see the girl and her friends ride on a one-track trolley, gliding along the ocean cliffs.
>
> I hear the croaking of frogs in the rice paddies on my way to school. I hear the endless humming of cicadas in our backyard. I hear opera from the neighborhood houses. I hear dogs barking and roosters crowing as the train rushes through the countryside. I smell the burning of incense in the tiny temple at the street corner, I smell the food cooking in front of the shops. It brings me back to a different world where I taste the fresh bamboo shoots, the world of untamed earth and unspoiled innocence.

No matter how the world has changed and will be changing, I can always find the past. I have relived my childhood through my grandchildren, through their eyes, their ears, and their hearts.

Her thoughts were interrupted as the light in the cabin was turned on, followed by the announcement, "Ladies and gentlemen, we are now approaching Seattle-Tacoma International Airport. Please be prepared for landing."

He Is the One

He was moving with the crowd in the airport security line, wearing a black jacket and a dark baseball cap. He turned around to look at her. His face turned pink with emotion. Tears flooded her eyeglasses.

He is the one who gave her the book of *Gilgamesh* when he learned that she, too, had lost a spouse to death. They shared their grief and opened their souls.

He is the one for whom she waited on the doorstep of her condo building. A slender figure under the New England summer sun, with a big smile on his face, he walked into her life.

He is the one who insisted that she was a beautiful woman. His eyes followed her wherever she went, be it at the end of the hallway or across the aisle in an auditorium. He is the one who, with his daily phone calls, made her heart sing. He is the one who, right after his surgery, walked toward her with wobbling steps but crushed her with an iron embrace and passionate kisses.

He is the one to whom she offered her heart and soul. The giant whale found his timid mermaid in a thundering cove. Together they rode on the waves in fairyland's coasts. He is the one who came to her in dreams, tenderly calling her, "My darling, my princess." She pressed him to her heart and kissed him on his head. As they walked side by side, she turned around, looking at his powerful profile. As they sat face to face, he gazed at her intently, totally absorbed in her expressions.

He is the one she wanted to be with, day or night, rain or shine. She would consult with him about what she should wear to a party. He would put on the shirt she chose for him just to rejoice in her smile of approval. He devoured every dish served on her dining table, even the broccoli, as long as it was cooked by her. They marveled at the city lights on the wintry rooftop and curled up to the warmth of each other.

He is the one who never ceased to be amazed by her talents and unique insights. He was the rock in her journey of self-discovery. They shared their minds through intense debates. He was proud of every word she said and every piece of work she created.

For years, they walked on the shifting sands by the ocean, on the trails knotty with tree roots, on the uneven pavement of the city streets. Their fingers were always locked together, as if hanging on to something tenuous.

Week after week, she looked forward to the weekend when he would come into her life, and she dreaded the emptiness left behind when the weekend was over. Week after week, he was torn between his yearning to be with his beloved and his commitment to his only child who depended on him for everything.

Autumn was setting in and the daylight became frightfully short. No one knew whether one would ever wake up to another spring. The migratory birds were tired of flying; the galloping horses turned away from the northerly wind. She yearned for a place on a branch up on the treetop that she could call home. And she wanted to return home to her children, the fruit of her lifelong toils.

He is the one who took her to the airport on the airport bus one early winter morning. She saw the Square in darkness, except for one Christmas tree with eerie lights of purple and white. They would never be here again to enjoy the ice sculptures lit up in the

Square as part of the city's year-end celebration. He spent all his waking hours thinking of her, only consoled by the prospect of visiting her three thousand miles away.

The security line kept moving. She waved faintly. "Sweetest one, I did not go because I loved you any less. My heart falls in pieces seeing you so haggard after months of separation. I cry at the thought of your silent weeping. But I know you will pull yourself through and carry on without me. Just remember the ecstasy we shared in our dreams, my dearest love, let the sparks of that encounter light up our separate paths ahead," she said silently as the man in the black jacket and dark baseball cap disappeared behind the security desk.

The Little Red House and Other Things Too

Like a fire engine, its bricks were painted
red and its frames shiny black.
Like a human face, it had two windows for eyes
and a single front door for a mouth.
I pushed your wheelchair by the little red house.
We picked up the blackberries before the
birds would have eaten them up.
You, with one injured leg,
I, with tender affection in my heart.

We walked by it whenever the wind
brought us into that direction.
Who lives in that little red house? I wondered.
It looks like a two-family condo, judging
by the common door, I said.
But it has three garages on the side, you said.
From the next street below, we found the answer.
A multi-level structure perched on the
hill overlooking the ravine.
Like the cliff dwellers, each family occupying
a plane on the sloped ground.
It greeted the sun in the morning,

it greeted the moon at night,
it greeted the trolley cars shuttling down below.
A guarding angel for all passersby.

Why did it come to my dream at dawn?
What if we were to live in a little red house like that?
But it was only a dream, and only in the dream
could we ever build our life together.

ㅇㄴ

We took the paths along the water's edge,
we took the paths between the mossy trunks.
You, looking for a secret spot,
I, looking out for you.
You led the way over the knotty roots,
I fought my way through tangled branches.
We found a special hideout,
a passage to our hearts' desire
away from human chatters and dog barking.
But we needed a fresh breath from the sea.
We lingered by the shimmering light from the bay.
We lost the spot as the sun went down.
The ferns grew over it as fleetingly as the sunset.

ㅇㄴ

On the desolate dock of Foss Point,
we found a respite from COVID.
Over the water from the dock,
the industrial compound spit smoke like a monster chimney.
It's certainly not the Christmas lights or
the Fourth of July fireworks
seen from your apartment on the hill.

We wobbled on the floating decks,
we walked by the empty parking lot.
We admired houseboats moored to the piers, agitated.
We saw kayaks gliding by at six feet apart.
We rejoiced at the tugboats breaking the water forward.

This is the real world, not an illusion from the top of the hill,
an open, remote, and worry-free world.
This is for us to enjoy but not to keep.
We enjoyed it while our world consisted of only you and me.
This is not an illusion but a real world,
only for the moment but not for eternity,
as one day the dock will float away, and the land dredged again.

I Cast a Last Glance from #2210

I see Mount Guanyin basking in the soft morning glow.
Silently she greets the sun and moon.
Silently she embraces the rain and thunder.
Silently she takes in the disruptions of humans.
Temples, footpaths, and high-rises dot her face.
A giant Boeing 777 drags its shadow over her back.
She is always there,
she greeted me as a little girl,
she greets me as a returning diaspora.
Silently she speaks to me like a true goddess,
with moving cloud for her crown.
Out of the quarantine,
out of the artificial bubble,
will I be free of the lingering past?
Will I be free of the illusion for the future?
Will I be serene like the mountain
with moving cloud for my crown?

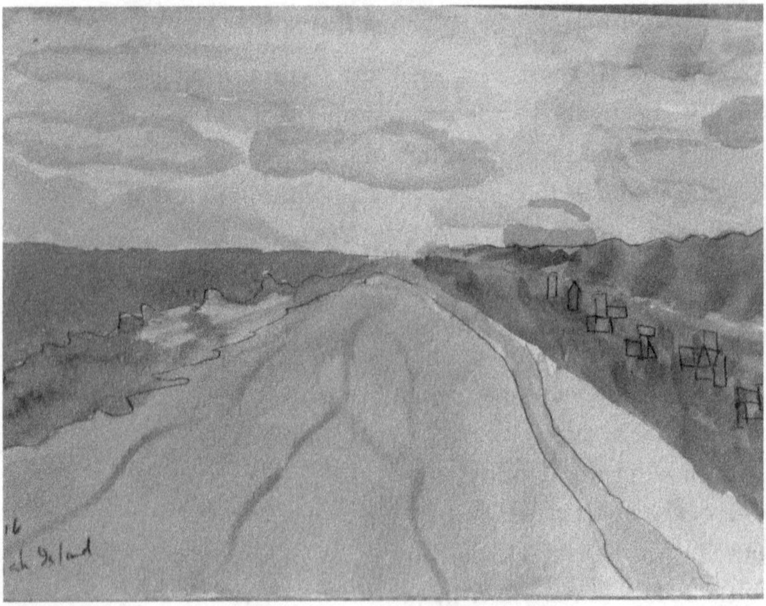

The Project

I led a solitary life after my wife's passing. My wife and I were married for twenty-seven years, and we had no children. Soon after she died, I went to Congo to work on a consulting assignment. Every day after work I walked to the beach and cried my head off. I missed her, I missed my beloved wife, I missed my constant companion. I was alone in this desolate and alien world. The waves were pounding on the shore as if pouring out the grief overfilled in my chest.

I met my wife in the mid-1950s when I was a member of the British Overseas Service in Hong Kong, and we got married three years later. We traveled together to wherever my job took me, be it a busy city like Rome or Bangkok, or an exotic country like Tanzania or Mauritius. I often thought it must be hard for her to be so far from her family. Yet she never complained about it even when she was gravely ill in the hospital. "Your wife said to me," her doctor told me later, "that she had a happy life, traveling all over the world." With her natural intelligence and poise, my wife always charmed the people we met and made friends wherever we were.

Now I was alone. I couldn't resist the impulse to go back home, the only place where I could still connect myself with her. Every Friday I left my office in Tilburg, Holland, and drove to the seaport to take an overnight ferry crossing the Channel. When the boat arrived in England near dawn, I would drive another couple of hours to reach home. By the time I arrived, it was almost the time for me to head back for Holland.

We had bought this duplex near the seaside resort of Brighton with the government payout when I left the Service to join a Dutch consulting firm. We lived there between my foreign assignments. How we rejoiced in having our own place after years of nomadic living in government housing! Now she was gone, and so was her smile, her slender figure on top of the stairs welcoming me home. All was quiet and empty now. Coming home only made me feel more homeless. Eventually I sold the place and moved to London.

As I settled into my widowerhood I found solace in music and walking. I wrote music in my spare time, something I had done since my early adulthood. I loved taking long walks through crowded streets in the city, or on the mountain paths between remote villages when I was on foreign assignments. I gradually became used to my solitary life and learned to like it.

As I approached my retirement I moved back to England and worked part-time for the same firm in Holland. Between my assignments I kept regular contact with my two cousins, one in London and the other in the countryside.

It was at this juncture that I met Tina. I was with my cousins and their families on a trip to Hong Kong. As one of the family guests, Tina was seated next to me in the restaurant. She was in her late twenties, attractive in an exotic way. She was a foreign exchange dealer at that time, constantly on the phone, even during the dinner. Nonetheless, this young woman and I struck up a cordial conversation. I found her not only lively but genuinely friendly. For several years since my wife died, I had missed being with the Chinese people. I warmed up to this young woman straightaway.

A year later I met her again in London, where she was visiting her boyfriend. With my long years in the Far East, we had a great deal to talk about. One thing led to the other, and we became friends. I was delighted to have a regular companion for a casual meal in the Chinese restaurants. She was an addition to my otherwise monotonous semi-retirement, almost like a daughter that I never had. My social circle was significantly enlarged as I made acquaintances in her circle, even though they were starkly different from the people I used to know and socialize with. I was attracted by the novelty and excitement of a different experience that I had never had in my early years.

For her I was a father figure to whom she confided her problems and issues. When she had a bitter split-up with her boyfriend, I lent a shoulder for her to cry on and provided my support as she needed. To make a life of her own in England, Tina ventured into the London property market. She bought two condo units in a nice neighborhood with an aim to turn them into rental units. I marveled at her energy and determination once I visited her amid remodeling, with wires dangling from the ceiling and maddening noise of the construction. I even helped her paint the interior walls. Apart from her obvious savviness in business, Tina impressed me with her many qualities, especially given her limited education and miserable childhood. Her vision of a new life was: "When my flats start to produce income, I'll use the money to buy another unit and get my sister over to study in a proper UK university."

One day, Tina stopped by, looking distressed.

"What's the matter?" I asked.

"My visa is expiring. The Immigration Department won't extend it, as I have already extended it twice."

Tina had come to England with a tourist visa in anticipation of getting married. Now she was split up with her boyfriend, she would be deported if she overstayed in the UK. For a while, she got away with it by paying hefty sums of tuition to an evening school for a three-month visa extension. Apparently, the Immigration Department wouldn't accept that anymore.

"I would have to go back to Hong Kong. You know how much I dread going back there! I came here to start a new life; how can I go back empty-handed?" She was in tears.

I felt terribly sorry seeing her in such distress. As I was on the eve of my departure for Africa, I could only assure her, "If there is anything I can do to help, please let me know."

When I returned from my assignment a few weeks later, she was in a better mood.

"I found this guy in Chinatown who is willing to marry me to get me the UK Permanent Residency (PR). Of course, it's all under contract; we will get a divorce as soon as I get my PR."

So, the project went on as planned, and for a while Tina thought she was immune from deportation. As time went on, the other party became more and more worried about the ever-increasing and rigorous ID investigations that he got cold feet and bailed out. So, the deal was off.

It didn't take Tina very long to find another deal: a man agreed to marry her but insisted that in addition to paying him a handsome sum of money, he and Tina would be living with his male companion under the same roof. Instinctively I felt it wasn't right. "You don't know those people, Tina. You could get yourself into a terrible situation!"

"What can I do, then?" After a short pause, she said, "My sister suggested that since I'm friendly with you, and you are someone I can trust, why don't you marry me to help me stay in England?"

"Sure," I answered. "I have pledged to help you. I'll marry you if that will pull you out of the impasse." Isn't that crazy that I would make a commitment of marriage without any hesitation? For me it was a matter of keeping my word more than anything else.

Decades before, it had taken three years for me to propose

marriage to my wife. In that era, it was socially unacceptable for an upper-class British person to marry a colonial subject, but it turned out to be the best thing I ever did in my life. This time it was a marriage of convenience for Tina to get her residency, not for me, as I had no desire to take advantage of her in her most vulnerable state. It wouldn't hurt anyone, and it would help a dear friend to make it in a foreign country. For all those years of my widowerhood, I had no illusion of getting married or sharing my life with someone again. What could I lose? She trusts me and counts on me for a major decision in her life. It was an act of charity on my part, and I sincerely believed that, even if legally incorrect, it was morally justified. Didn't W. H. Auden do the same for Thomas Mann's daughter, Erika?

"Oh, no, I cannot do that!" Tina quickly stepped back. "I regard you as my honorary uncle. How can I put you through that? It's my problem, I just have to resolve it on my own."

So, the matter was dropped. During the intervening months Tina returned to Hong Kong and came back with a fresh visa that allowed her to stay in England for ninety days.

"I cannot go on like this forever," she said when we met for dinner in a Chinese restaurant.

I nodded.

"Do you remember your offer to help me get the citizenship?" She looked at me under the dim light in the restaurant. "Is it still open?"

"Yes, I'll keep my pledge to you as long as you keep this arrangement from my family," I replied.

We got married. I was sixty-six, she was thirty-three. With so much unknown ahead I was rather nervous, and equally excited, like what I always experienced when I embarked on a new assignment. But this time the endeavor was far more complex than a consulting project. It was a real-life adventure!

To create credible evidence for the Immigration Department,

we held a small wedding reception at a fancy restaurant and took many pictures. Immediately after the wedding, a lawyer was hired for the application of Tina's UK Permanent Residency.

To maintain the fiction as though the marriage were consummated, Tina moved in with me. She had the guest room and a separate bath, with her own telephone line. We maintained a landlord-tenant relationship with different daily routines. Every day I got up early to write music and prepare my own meals. Her day usually didn't start until noon. Sometimes, she cooked a meal and invited me to join her. So, it went as well as it could be, but not for very long.

Then she began to bring her friends over, men as well as women. She gave parties on the rooftop of my penthouse duplex. "You are, of course, invited as our honorary guest," so I couldn't turn down her plans. I tried to convince myself, "After all, I let her live here, she should be able to live the way she wishes." After a while, with all the drinking, smoking, and late-night outings, it became arduous for me, but I still couldn't admit to myself that it had been a mistake to let her move in, or to marry her, for that matter.

Meanwhile, as the sponsor for her PR, I had to hand in my passport and other official documents to the Immigration Department. Not being able to travel, I lost my part-time job with the consulting firm. I felt trapped. My only respites were occasional visits to my cousins who could no longer stay with me as I had lost the use of my guest room. This commitment proved to be far more difficult than what had been expected. I couldn't even talk about my ordeal with my family as no one could know that I was married to Tina.

Deep inside me, I realized it was a folly that I did to myself, like one of those silly episodes that often occurred to men going through a second adolescence. Nevertheless, I regarded this marriage as a moral obligation, not just a legally binding arrangement.

In reality, I bore all the responsibilities as her legal spouse. One late evening Tina and her party went out after some drinks. She was trapped by her long skirt and fell from the stairs. She was taken to the hospital, and I was the one staying all night in the waiting room for her release while all her fair-weather friends disappeared on her. As my lawful wife, she was on my health insurance and credit cards. To her credit, Tina usually settled the accounts with me for her expenses charged on my credit. She wanted to be respected as a person with scruples in financial matters.

The first step for Tina's PR application went through in a few months. She got a one-year residency which allowed her to live in the UK and to work if she opted for it. But that was only the first step. There were two more years for the full PR to be granted. I could only bite the bullet, hoping the process would go through without further episodes.

But it was not so easy for Tina. Not hearing from the Immigration Department for a while, she lost her patience. From time to time she lashed out at me or went into a thundering rage for whatever I said or did that was not to her liking. Living with her was like sailing on the sea. It could be calm in one moment and stormy the next, but one would never know when that storm would appear. Occasionally she got into a fit of temper and smashed dishes on the ground. As always, she would come to me later with tears and apologies. "You are the best person I've ever met ... Do you know I love you more than my own parents?"

As time went on, I found myself nonetheless attached to (or rather used to) her existence in my day-to-day life. For better or for worse, she filled the emotional void left by my wife. If I went shopping in Chinatown, I'd always bring back something for her. When she behaved abominably, I would try to find excuses for her, thinking, "Well, she is young, living here is just too boring for her." There were days when we got along on good terms. We would talk at great length, in most instances over a bottle of wine. Our conversation would always end up with her many boyfriends. "I'm fond of Steve but he is using me ... I'm afraid I got too close to Anthony ... Tim is a sweet kid but ..." I only hoped that whomever she should end up with would treat her well, but I rather doubted that.

As the first year ground into the second, while I struggled to carry on with this "project" as best as I could, my domestic life was turning into a nightmare. From time to time, Tina spent the night with her lovers. I told her in vain that she was free to do whatever she wanted, but not in my place. With my sanctuary violated and my honor tarnished, I decided to stop living with her while continuing my sponsorship of her citizenship. But how should I ask her to move out? She would say, "You promised to get me the UK citizenship. Now you are pulling the plug on me!" One never knew what Tina could do when she was desperate and angry. What if she let Immigration know the truth of the marriage, would I be charged for violating the law? I must go gentle on this. The only way to get her out of the place was to sell it. And it worked. She moved back to her own flat, and I was greatly relieved when I found another flat in the center of London and was living there by myself again.

We still saw each other regularly, having a drink or meal together while counting down the days for the official decision regarding her PR application.

In the spring before I turned sixty-nine, entirely out of the blue, my fate turned in the opposite direction on me.

I met Jane, a business consultant from the States who had lost her husband a year earlier. We made our acquaintance in one of my overseas assignments. We were reconnected when she came to

London on one of her business trips. Soon we found a soul mate in each other.

What should I do and what could I do?

If I told Jane the truth, she would most likely leave me, let alone wait five more years for me to be free of this entangled mess. Once Tina got the promised citizenship, that would be the end of our relationship and I'd lead my life in solitude again, taking walks in solitude, eating daily meals in solitude, until I fade away in solitude.

For almost five years, Tina had been a constant fixture in my life. Now I found Jane with whom I wish to share a meaningful relationship and a normal family life for as long as I live. If I dropped Tina now, who knows what she would do to cause all sorts of trouble. After all, it was my own doing to carry on with this crazy "project" with her. How could I have a clear conscience if I broke my pledge with one woman in pursuit of another?

It was almost the end of three years; Tina should hear from the ID regarding her full PR any time, which would allow her to stay in the UK indefinitely. Perhaps she would be good enough to release me from the marriage, perhaps not.

All those years in my widowerhood, I had no illusion of sharing life with someone again. I entered the arrangement with Tina because I thought it wouldn't hurt anyone and would help a friend in need. In the end, the only one hurt was no one but me.

Letter from Jakarta

My first overseas assignment with Price Waterhouse was in Jakarta, Indonesia, in the fall of 1990. I was the only Asian in this USAID-funded project.

While I had been brought up in Taiwan, only a few hours' flight from Jakarta, going to Indonesia didn't feel like homecoming to me, nor did I have the exotic notion of an island paradise that seemed prevalent among my peers. All I knew about the country was from a couple of scientist friends of my husband, who were among the Chinese who repatriated to China from Indonesia in the 1950s. Their grievance about the country was its legislation excluding Chinese Indonesians since the time of the Dutch East Indies. Ethnic Chinese were required to always carry a special pass. After independence, the Sukarno regime further expanded this policy prohibiting Chinese Indonesians from doing business outside of urban areas.

I was also told by our friends that "the Indonesians are lazy, staying idle all day long. When they are hungry, they eat bananas, which can be found everywhere; when they are tired, they take a bath in the stream, wash their clothes and hang them on the branches while taking a nap ..." In this environment, the Chinese must have had a tough time reconciling their traditional values with the lifestyle of Indonesians. I wondered how things had changed in the ensuing decades.

One thing I knew that remained unchanged was the pervasive anti-Chinese sentiment among the Indonesians. As the Chinese work ethics did not mix with the local culture, it's conceivable that discrimination, distrust, and violence against Chinese Indonesians were caused in part by a perception that they were unwilling to mingle with other ethnic groups.

On the last leg of my flight to Jakarta, in the first-class cabin, I noticed a cast of passengers quite different from what one would normally encounter. They were glamorous-looking Asian ladies wearing open-toe high heels with no bags strapped on their delicate shoulders, and businessmen conversing in Hakka dialect or Mandarin Chinese. After we landed in the Jakarta airport, a fleet of Mercedes ranging in color from cream to jet black and driven by uniformed chauffeurs, steadily moved up the ramp, and then off went the Chinese businessmen. Apparently, the

Chinese are not doing too badly in Indonesia; that was my instant reflection.

Next morning, I woke up to the sound of a baby crying. I walked outside my room in Borobudur Hotel, only to find a tropical bird making a noise like a baby crying! Borobudur was not just a hotel, but a holiday compound equipped with six tennis and basketball courts and a full-size tropical bird aviary. In the early morning light, with the soft breeze between colorful flowers and lush greens, I saw Indonesian gardeners moving about to the rhythms of trimming, mowing, and sweeping. The sweat over their bodies made their skin shine like bronze.

How different this was from what I saw the day before on my ride from the airport! Dusty country roads with makeshift huts and banana stalls, slums against a backdrop of high-rises crowded with people staring into empty space with dark and deep-set eyes.

Around noon, the dozen or so restaurants in the hotel were filled with guests who came to enjoy a Sunday brunch after working out on the sports grounds and a splash in the pools. It was obvious that these were the privileged class of a country rich in oil and other natural resources. And these people looked like Chinese to me. What have the Chinese done to reach such social status and prosperity given all the political persecution and discrimination over all the country those years? I didn't have the answer until I came across an article about the New Order imposed by President Suharto:

> For some prominent Chinese businessmen who were friends of Suharto, the New Order was a bonanza: they received huge government contracts and became some of the richest men in Asia.

I rarely went out during my six-month sojourn in Jakarta. On weekdays, I went to the office with an American colleague who had a chauffeured car. On weekends, I went shopping with his wife. One day, I decided I would venture into the city by myself. As I waited outside the hotel, a taxi sped up and stopped right in front of me. When the driver leaned over to open the window on my side, his expression changed from eagerness to reluctance and then something like disgust. To my total shock, he immediately rolled up the window and sped away as quickly as he came. What is this? Is this because I'm Chinese? I certainly looked Chinese, as I am taller and fairer, among the Indonesians. When I told my friend and his wife about this, they became worried and insisted that I should always go out in their chauffeured car.

Before I left Jakarta for the last time, I took a one-day tour arranged by the hotel. As I waited in a nineteen-seat van, a group of Japanese businessmen streamed in, followed by a few foreign tourists and a mother with her adult daughter. The ladies were ethnic Chinese, recognizable by their conversation in Fujian dialect. Once the tour started, the daughter went over to join the Japanese. She had no problem gaining their acceptance with her fluent Japanese—most Chinese in Indonesia are multilingual. As the day went on, the van made several sightseeing stops. The younger Chinese woman was most diligent in interpreting for the Japanese. It was apparent that she had her eyes on one of them, a rather handsome man of her own age. Toward the end of the tour, the friendship turned intimate; the two sat side by side, totally oblivious to others.

Meanwhile, I noticed the mother, who sat by herself, completely indifferent to what was going on with her daughter. I moved to the seat across the aisle from her and the two of us quickly struck up a conversation. I learned that her family had been in Indonesia for generations, and she herself was the owner of a business in a city ninety kilometers from Jakarta.

"Is it difficult for the Chinese to do business in Indonesia with all the government restrictions?" I asked.

"Well, we manage alright. We bring business to the country and jobs to the people. I don't see why they should treat us too badly."

"It's truly remarkable how the Chinese in Indonesia still maintain their traditions," I commented. "Most Chinese Indonesians are fluent in Chinese, even among the second and third generations."

That subject seemed to open a floodgate in her. "We used to have Chinese schools in every city of the country. Unfortunately, that was abolished by the government since Suharto took power in 1965, even though most Chinese Indonesians over thirty are still conversant in Chinese, and the Chinese language is still in use by most media."

Hearing this, I said, "It seems there is a large Chinese community where you live."

"Yes, but it's getting harder and harder for the Chinese population in Indonesia. The Chinese are not allowed to keep their ethnic identity, even their names. The Chinese must change their family names." This reminded me of a Chinese Indonesian couple, both physicians practicing in London, whose surname sounded more Indian than Chinese. It also made me wonder as to how the country could retain talented professionals under such exclusion policies.

After a while, I switched the subject. "Are marriages between the Chinese and non-Chinese common?"

"Yes, quite common, particularly among the younger generations," she said. "In most cases, it's between the Chinese and other foreign nationalities. Marriages between Chinese and Indonesians are rare."

My curiosity was piqued. "How many children do you have? To whom are they married?"

"I have another daughter who married a Dutchman; she couldn't find a Chinese husband."

"Do you mind if your daughter finds a Japanese husband?"

She shrugged. "It would certainly beat having an Indonesian for a son-in-law."

In the twilight of the day, the van stopped at the hotel where the Japanese stayed. After bidding farewell to her newly acquainted friend, and with much sorrow in her voice, the young lady took the seat next to her mother without saying a single word.

In May of 1998, as the Suharto regime limped to an ignominious end, riots erupted in areas of cities predominantly populated by ethnic Chinese. More than 1,200 people died, dozens of women were raped, and hundreds of shops were burned to the ground...Yet, the ethnic Chinese community is starting to rediscover its confidence and beginning to take advantage of the democratic reforms that have swept through the country over the past seven years. In some ways the rise of China has been a vital part of this process.

BBC News, 3 March 2005, Chinese Diaspora: Indonesia by Tim Johnston

I have never returned to Indonesia since that assignment in 1990. That experience helped me understand more deeply the issues with the Chinese diaspora in general, and my own identify. I know I'm always Chinese wherever I go.

Out of the End of the World

Seven of us and a bodyguard sat in the van and the engine had been running idle for a while. What are we waiting for? Everyone had the same question but remained politely silent as we stared out of the widow nervously. Time seemed to stand still. We needed the driver to take us back to the city after a day trip to the park. But where was the driver?

When we started the trip in the morning I was musing on the name of the park, "Tian Ya Hai Jiao" ("The Tip of Heaven and the Corner of the Sea"), as it was indeed on the southernmost tip of Hainan Island, the southernmost territory of China in the South China Sea.

Now I wondered if this place was more isolated than poetic as its name suggested. A sense of alienation started to creep in. Where was the driver? We needed him to take us back to the city.

That was in the winter of 1994. I was working on a project as a foreign consultant for the People's Bank of China, the central bank of China. From time to time, customary to local practice, the bank organized off-site conferences in scenic places around the country. This time the conference was held in this "island paradise" of Hainan. As part of non-business activity, the bank gave us a tour of this famous park on the southern tip of the island. They deployed two vehicles for the trip: a full-size bus for the thirty-plus Chinese officials attending the conference and a fourteen-seater van for the foreign consultants, myself included. The van was brand-new, bought just for this trip.

After spending a few hours in the park, we were ready to return to the city for lunch. Then, where was the driver? He was apparently arguing with the gatekeeper who stopped us from exiting the park.

"The ticket on the windshield is for the locals." The gatekeeper interrogated the driver as the car tried to move through the gate. "Why didn't you pay the foreign rate for entrance admission?"

Since the economic reform started in the 1980s, a duo system was practiced in China. Foreigners were charged a higher fee for all events and places. In this case, the entrance fee was 35 yuan for each foreigner and 2.50 for a Chinese. The exchange rate then was about eight yuan to one dollar.

"What do you mean that we should pay the foreign rate?" our driver retorted.

The gatekeeper came out of the gatehouse, threw his cigarette on the ground, and smeared it forcefully with the flip-flop on his one foot as if showing the world that he could crash anybody like a bunch of ants. "The car is full of *lao-wei* (good old foreigners). You must pay the foreign rate for each of them to get out of here."

"They are the guests of the People's Bank of China; we have a special permit for them."

"*Hushuo* (bullshit)! This rule is for everyone. I won't let you go unless you pay the difference." The gatekeeper showed no sign of budging.

"Can you read this?" The driver got off the van from his side and waved the paper in front of the gatekeeper.

From my vantage point in the van, I saw two menacing figures facing each other, our driver, a lightweight young man in uniform, and the gatekeeper, a rough-looking middle-aged man, shouting as he raised one forefinger right to the face of his challenger, as if to say, "PAY IT OR ELSE." Their voices grew louder and the air more intense with each suggestive body language. Yet no one in the van would do anything to interfere.

Suddenly, right before my eyes, a group of what seemed to be more than one hundred people emerged. It was entirely beyond my imagination as to where these people came from on this very end of the earth. As the group got closer to the gate, it took no time for our driver and the gatekeeper to disappear into the crowd. Just at this moment, before we could stop it, our own bodyguard jumped out of the car from his side of the van and raced toward the crowd.

When we started out our excursion in the morning, it took me by surprise that a bodyguard was in the car with us. He was a slender young man in military (or paramilitary) attire, with a pistol by the side of his waist. He looked serious and was as taciturn as a bodyguard was supposed to be, and we made no effort to chat with him either. I didn't know why we needed a bodyguard, let alone a skinny fellow like this one. But Director Li at the bank had assured us that it was only customary to have a guard for the foreign visitors in Hainan.

Hainan, as a primitive and remote territory in the southernmost part of the country, was known historically as the place for political convicts in the past century. This was still the case during the initial years of the Communist regime in China. Many overseas Chinese returning to China were sent there for hard labor. As a consequence, Hainan gained a notorious reputation for its high crime rate. In any case, we now realized why the bank had to deploy a security guard for us.

But we now lost both our driver and guard. In front of us was a mob, a cacophony of shouting and the commotion of people pushing against each other. Amid all that, suddenly, a series of sharp sounds "Pop … pop, pop …" were piercing through the air. We looked at each other in horror. Were those gunshots? Was that from our bodyguard or the police? Deputy Director Madame Xu, our host and leader, turned white like a sheet of paper.

Madame Xu was the right-hand person for Director Li, the bank official in charge of the World Bank Project we worked on. Before the trip, she had warned us not to mingle with the locals, saying, "You will encounter herds of vendors in the park. Just pretend you don't understand them. Don't even look at the stuff they sell." By her implication, the locals were known to be lawless, and the local police was simply toothless and they could even side with the locals.

The agitation of the crowd didn't abate to the sound of gunshots. Instead, more people surfaced. It was a real mobster scene now!

BUT WHERE IS OUR DRIVER?

One member of our team, a man from California, shouted, "Let's go!" Within a split second, like a lightning bolt he dashed over to the driver's seat and the car started to move forward.

"Go! ... Go!" we shouted in unison.

Like a miracle unfolding in front of my own eyes, the car sailed through the gate without any glitches and moved along the highway, winding along the coast. We didn't know where we were going but this was the only way exiting the park. The car curved along the edge of the land where deep blue waves reached the horizon with shimmering lights under the warm sunlight of the South China Sea.

It can't be that easy! Ferocious shouting was behind us, and through the rear window I saw a group of people frantically running after the car like wild animals running for their lives.

"Faster, faster ... they are after us!" someone shouted.

The car sped up and the distance between us and the chasers quickly grew. Before the chasers dropped out of sight, they threw rocks at us in a furious frenzy, as if giving their best parting shots.

We kept driving beyond the cliff for what seemed like

three-quarters of an hour. When we reached a wooded area, we stopped the car and waited for the driver. All was quiet; it was hard to believe what had happened only moments earlier. It was even harder to believe when the driver appeared at the end of the road, limping along with only one shoe on his feet but otherwise no visible body injuries. He drove us back to the hotel without a single word, apparently very sulky. For the sake of proper protocol, none of us raised any questions either.

We had our lunch in the hotel as planned, but no one except us seemed to be worried about the bodyguard and the busload of bank staff who were left behind. After what seemed forever, a bus pulled into the hotel driveway and our bodyguard was in it with the rest of the bank staff. Except for a few bruises, he seemed unharmed. The only real damage was the rear window of our brand-new Toyota van which was unmistakably cracked. Well, it was bought with the World Bank money appropriated for the project anyway.

We had no idea as to how or whether this conflict was resolved but we solemnly promised Madame Xu not to mention this incident to anyone; it was more a sign of losing face for the bank than anything else.

Today, Hainan to the Chinese is what Hawaii is to the American tourists, a popular vacation resort. I wonder how the local resentment toward foreigners during those early years of economic reform has evolved. The duo system has been abolished since then. More importantly, the great surplus of human resources in the countryside—and, more importantly, its unleashed energy—have been channeled into the factories in the cities, thanks to the stewardship of Mr. Zhu Rongji, the Chinese vice premier and fifth premier from 1998 to 2003, who valiantly averted the possible catastrophic effects of the economic reform. I remember with pride that he was the chairman of the People's Bank of China which I served as a foreign consultant from 1993 to 1995.

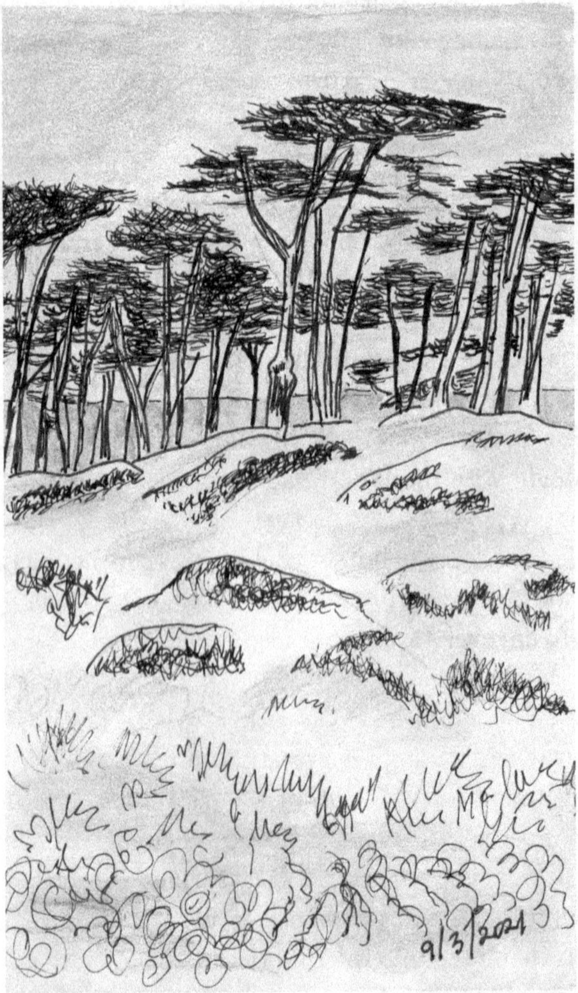
9/3/2021

Pakistan Diary

Parents Know Better
December 1992, Lahore, Pakistan

Most marriages in Pakistan are arranged by parents. This system works and is necessary in an environment where young people are kept from direct contact with the opposite sex, and children of all ages are closely tied to the parents' families.

I asked the wives of some of my Pakistan colleagues how they liked their arranged marriages. The answer was invariably, "Our parents know better; we can trust them to choose the most suitable husbands for us."

Imran was married to the daughter of a Cabinet member of Nawaz Sharif, the then-Prime Minister. I asked him how his marriage had been arranged. He said, "My father had a friend who knew my father-in-law. He introduced the two of them to each other; my father made a proposal for marriage, and it was accepted." His answer sounded surprisingly easy or even indifferent for an important matter such as this.

"Didn't you know each other, your future wife and yourself?"

"When the proposal was made, we were introduced to each other. Neither of us had any objection, so we were engaged to marry." They had two babies in quick succession only two years into their marriage.

"What if the parties find out later their marriage doesn't work?" I asked Imran's wife when I was invited to their home.

"If the marriage doesn't work out," she assured me, "all the wife needs to do is to say, 'I divorce you, I divorce you, I divorce you,' three times in public. The marriage will then be annulled." I couldn't challenge the legality of this practice, but I wondered how women not belonging to the privileged class would walk out on their marriages, given that most of them couldn't support themselves. Nor did I know if they would have the right to keep their children. Nonetheless, I must admit the divorce rate was extremely low in Pakistan. The wives I had met seemed content with their husbands and their roles in the family.

The project director's wife, who ran a home factory making children's garments with her sister, told me that "the Pakistani women enjoy a better and stronger bond with each other than their counterparts in the West; they don't have to compete for men." I found this view revealing as to how conventional dating was regarded by people here. It seemed that engaging in dating activity was too much trouble to be worth the time and energy. Yet, I wondered how keen the competition among the parents in Pakistan must be for finding "the suitable spouses" for their children, as very few people would have the kind of connection that Irman's father had.

About that time, I was invited to the wedding of a Pakistani colleague's son, a three-day affair with hundreds of guests. I sat on the right side of the hall with all the female guests while the male guests sat on the opposite side. The groom and the parents from both sides sat on a sofa on the stage facing the audience, waiting for the beautiful bride to walk up the aisle with her entourage. The lady next to me told me the groom was an engineering student in the States and his bride was a trained physician in Pakistan. The marriage had been arranged long-distance. They planned to go back to the States after the wedding. Nowadays, most still choose to find their spouse through the traditional approach, even those educated in the West.

At the end of December, when we planned a business trip to Karachi, Irfan, my twenty-three-year-old assistant, was thrilled that he would accompany me on the trip. "Irfan's fiancée lives in Karachi," Imran told me.

Bashfully, Irfan showed me a four-by-six photo of a young girl, fully made up and dressed up, adorned with jewelry over her face, head, neck and arms.

"She is as beautiful as a princess in a fairy tale," I commented. "When will you get married?"

"She is only sixteen. We will be married when she is out of girls' school."

"Do you get to see her often?" I asked.

"She is my cousin. I will see her when I pay visits to her parents."

A good portion of marriages in Pakistan are within the families. "Keep the rich water from spilling into your neighbors' fields," just like the traditional Chinese thinking.

"Could you suggest something I can bring on our upcoming trip?" he asked me.

I suggested a flask of name-brand perfume.

"GREAT IDEA!" he exclaimed. "I'll ask my mother to buy it tonight." He couldn't wait to go home.

"The lad is in love," I thought. I was not sure whether he "fell" in love or "walked" into it, but I knew he was clearly in love, and with the one who was going to be his mate for life.

Changing of Guards
December 1992, Lahore, Pakistan

It was the political season in Pakistan. I saw demonstrations on my way to the Audit Department. Benazir Bhutto was the opposition party candidate challenging the incumbent Prime Minister Nawaz Sharif. One day after work, upon entering the lobby of the hotel I stayed, I was blocked by a moving crowd. Amid an entourage of all colors, shapes, and general murmurs of excitement, a figure caught my eye, like a crane standing among chickens, shrouded in translucent white with a face dazzling all onlookers. It was Benazir. The next day, I read in the newspaper that she was at Avari, the hotel where I was staying, giving a talk to a special interest group. Bhutto had been the prime minister four years earlier, as the first woman prime minister in a Muslim country. She was ousted in 1990 on corruption charges. This was her first comeback after spending a few years in exile.

When the project administrator heard that I had seen Bhutto, his round eyes lit up instantly in their bony sockets. "She is my candidate, educated at Harvard and Oxford, a reform-minded leader. She's what we need."

"What are the most urgent issues facing Pakistan?" I asked.

"Among other things, the conflicts between Pakistan and India are something the government must tackle sooner or later. India has become so much stronger, posing real threats to Pakistan. While the two nations currently maintain the status quo, the problem will eventually erupt out of proportion." He went on to suggest that I visit the changing of the guards at the border, about thirty minutes outside of Lahore.

The changing of the guards at the Pakistan-India border was different from that at the Vatican or Buckingham Palace, yet like the others, it is a tourist attraction, set at the summit of a park where families picnic on the lawn with little children toddling or running around. As the sun, like a giant fireball, was about to set between the two mountain ranges in the west, the waiting crowd began to move toward the area where the changing of guards was to take place. The area, about one hundred feet long, was paved with cement and with flower beds planted around its edges. Iron gates with grids in the middle of the paved area demarcated the boundary of the two countries. The gates opened automatically at the shout of the commanders toward each side, signifying the beginning of the ceremony. Two teams of dark, handsome soldiers in their highly ornate ceremonial uniforms, Pakistanis in dark green and Indians in brown, with peacock-style headgear, walked in, long guns on their shoulders. The respective teams took turns exercising the maneuvers, kicking their disproportionally long legs to the position almost parallel to the ground, twisting their torsos deliberately while making a ninety-degree turn. Their boots stomped on the pavement crisply, the long guns flew from one hand to the other in unison. After marching to the opposite end of the pavement, the teams returned to their respective territories. Without any hesitation, the iron gates closed behind them. All the while, the audience burst into applause as the sun quickly retreated behind the mountain ranges.

Benazir Bhutto won the election that year and became the prime minister for the second time, from 1993 to 1996. I was saddened by her assassination in 2007, and I wonder why in this "land of the pure" ("Paki" means "God" and "-stan" means "the land" in Urdu and Farci), political guardianship can mean changing hands through violent means.

On the Khyber Pass
December 1992, Peshawar, Pakistan

I always had romantic notions about the Khyber Pass. According to the legend, it was where Alexander the Great made the crossing in his long expedition to conquer the East. I didn't dream that I would be there one day and see it with my own eyes.

When I completed the draft implementation plan for Pakistan's nationwide audit system, the deputy auditor general requested that I seek "buy-ins" from the provincial level officials. For my trip to North West Frontier Province (NWFP), I was accompanied by Mr. Khan, the project coordinator. On our way to Peshawar, the capital of NWFP, Mr. Khan told me, "The provincial auditor general is very pleased that you will come all the way to talk to him. He made special arrangements for you to stay in the summer house of the NWFP governor who is currently out of the country—there are no decent hotels in Peshawar, you know."

We were picked up at the Peshawar airport and were taken to the house directly. The car arrived at a ranch house on the hill after a half-hour drive on winding mountain roads. We were greeted by the servants at the front gate and led through a tree-lined path to the house. After giving brief instructions to the servants in Urdu, Mr. Khan left.

Now I was alone in a house somewhere totally unknown and mysterious. I walked around from room to room. Sofas and chairs were fitted with cotton covers stiff with starch. Everything was still except the big clock on the wall which made a steady tick-tock sound. I went to the garden and stood among rows of neatly planted flowers and vegetables. The setting sun on the faraway mountain ranges cast a pink hue on the land. The banana trees swayed their lush green arms in the evening breeze. When dinner was ready, I was led to the dining room facing a courtyard full of tropical plants and flowers. Dishes were brought in one by one: roasted leg of lamb, home-baked naan, stewed vegetables, spiced yogurt, freshly picked fruit, and mango ice cream. I was both enchanted and bewildered. "Is this real or am I in a dream?" I wondered.

The following morning, after a successful meeting, the auditor general asked me, "Let me know, Madam, where in NWFP you want to visit, I will be obliged."

Without any hesitation, I said, "Can I visit Khyber Pass?" not knowing the area around Khyber Pass was closed to foreign passport holders.

The provincial auditor general said he would try his best to get special permission for his distinguished guest. I didn't know it was the risky traffic of drug trade that made this area unsafe.

An assistant came back with the permit after a few hours. A motorcade, which consisted of a four-door sedan and a Toyota mini pickup truck, was waiting. Four guards with rifles on their shoulders sat on the back of the Toyota. Mr. Khan, the provincial assistant, and I were comfortably installed in the sedan. With the Toyota leading the way, we took off to the Khyber Pass border station some ninety kilometers west of Peshawar on the Afghanistan-Pakistan border.

The Safed Koh range that separates the two nations didn't appear as rugged as I had imagined for the mountain ranges in central Asia. The surrounding terrain was mostly barren. Occasional villages appeared in the landscape. Between the villages, people like small dots walked in single file on the muddy roads. The convoy moved steadily on the winding mountain road, slowing down only at checkpoints. The provincial assistant opened the window and waved a piece of paper in his hand and shouted a few words in Urdu to the guard. When I expressed my wish to take photos along the way, the entire convoy stopped. The four guards would spring to the ground from the back of the Toyota before I stepped out of the sedan, ready to stand on four sides of their charge with their rifles pointing outward.

I noticed cement blocks as big as a small house implanted in the ground as the cars approached the border in an area that stretched for several miles. Mr. Khan explained, "During the Soviet invasion, Pakistan built defenses on the ground to prevent the Soviets from coming in on their tanks. During those ten years, the Soviets exhausted their resources which eventually led to the disintegration of the Soviet Union. The Americans didn't give us due credit for winning the Cold War."

I didn't comment on what he said. I knew full well how I was regarded by my Pakistani colleagues: "She is a Chinese lady. China is always a true friend to Pakistan because it is often at odds with India."

When we arrived at the border station, we were ushered into the office and received the usual courtesy by the station master, with refreshments and tea. A small group of local people were waiting outside when I stepped out of the building. "The village people heard a Chinese lady is visiting us. They asked me to pass on their invitations for tea to you," explained the station master. A little girl snuck in and pulled my sleeves, her large black eyes staring at this strange Chinese lady.

Looking around, I saw mud huts and sheds built with makeshift materials. Dim lights and TV sounds came from within, and chickens, dogs, and goats wandered about outside. The facial features of the people here were different from those of average Pakistanis. Their sharp nostrils and fair skin tone, coupled with bent backs in ragged robes, bony shoulders wrapped in dirty shawls, and faces full of wrinkles under their cloth headgear, struck me as a perfect portrait of people in biblical times.

There was no border control on the road leading to Afghanistan. People came and went freely. Mr. Khan said, "The people of Afghanistan are our brothers. During the Soviet invasion, Pakistan absorbed over three million Afghan refugees. Some of them are returning to their homeland."

A truck went by carrying on its flatbed a couple of chairs and a goat standing on shaky legs. A few hundred meters farther stood the official monument of the Khyber Pass. It was a brick structure like a medieval castle gate, constructed in the twentieth century. In a stone tableau laid in the wall of the castle gate, the history of the Khyber Pass was inscribed in Urdu and English. I asked one of my escorts to take a photo of me in front of the sign. I bid goodbye to my gracious hosts, saying, "I'm so glad that I have seen the Khyber Pass."

They looked much relieved when the cars began our return journey.

On Khyber Pass with Afghan locals, 1991

CPSIA information can be obtained
at www.ICGtesting.com
Printed in the USA
BVHW081901150222
629079BV00004B/280

9 781665 714594

Nancy C Jacobson